THIS COOKBOOK IS THE

PROPERTY OF

Table of Contents

KITCHEN CONVERSIONS

American Legion Auxiliary

In the spirit of Service, Not Self, the **mission** of the **American Legion Auxiliary** is to support The **American Legion** and to honor the sacrifice of those who serve by enhancing the lives of our veterans, military, and their families, both at home and abroad.

The ALA Unit 148 plans events to help Veterans, to raise awareness of Americanism and support our military when and wherever needed.

The group gives away poppies, raises money to do special events for Veterans and helps with flag education in the schools. The ALA ladies have wrapped gifts, helped with bean suppers, and held nationally recognized Naturalization Ceremonies.

The Naturalization Ceremonies welcome new American citizens. The ALA gives scholarships to seniors and volunteers for local concert series in the summer.

The ALA is always looking for opportunities to help Veterans and to build their membership because there is power in greater numbers.

Emergency and Household Tips

Food and Water in an Emergency

- The rule of thumb is one gallon per person, per day, minimum, according to the Federal Emergency Management Agency.
- Never ration water.

How to Store Water

- Store your water in thoroughly washed plastic, glass, fiberglass or enamel-lined metal containers. You can also purchase food-grade plastic buckets.
- Make sure the water is sealed tightly and labeled before storing in a cool, dark place.
- Rotate every six months.

Emergency Outdoor Water Sources

- If you need water, you can use rainwater, streams, rivers and other moving water, ponds and lakes and natural springs. You can also melt snow in northern areas.
- Avoid water with floating material, an odor or dark color. - Do not drink flood water.

Purify Water

- Boil it. Bring water to a rolling boil for three to five minutes.
- Disinfect it. You can kill microorganisms with bleach that contains 5.25 percent sodium hypochlorite. *Don't use scented bleaches, color safe bleaches or bleach with additional cleaners.

Storage Tips

- Keep food in a cool, dry place
- Keep food covered
- Wrap cookies and crackers in plastic bags and keep them in tight containers
- Use foods before they go bad and inspect them before use. Use a rotating system with new items in back and older items in front. Date them with a marker.
- Don't refrigerate – Tomatoes, potatoes, onions, bread, bananas
- Read the storage recommendations on packaged foods.
- Buying dented cans is okay as long as the can isn't leaking. If there's a ring under the can, skip it, it might mean it's open.
- Nutrition Tips
- Eat at least one balanced meal per day
- Drink two quarts of water, at least, per day
- Get enough calories to do what you need to do
- Include vitamin supplements to get all nutrients
- Read the storage recommendations on packaged foods.
- Buying dented cans is okay as long as the can isn't leaking. If there's a ring under the can, skip it, it might mean it's open.

Nutrition Tips

 * Eat at least one balanced meal per day
- Drink two quarts of water, at least, per day
- Get enough calories to do what you need to do
- Include vitamin supplements to get all nutrients

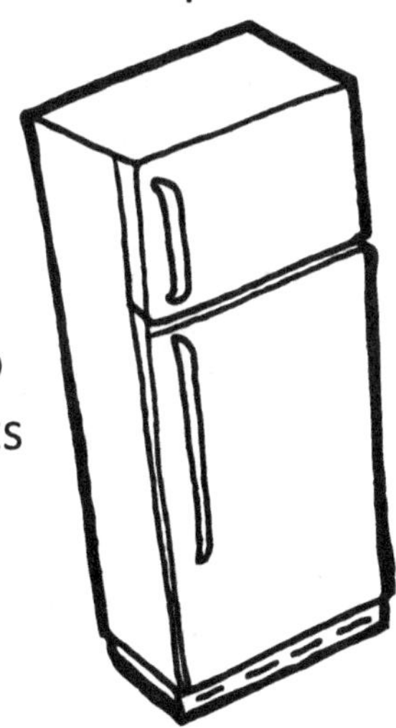

Shelf life for foods

- **Six months:** Powdered milk (boxed), dried fruit, dry, crisp crackers, potatoes
- **One Year:** Canned condensed meat and vegetable soups, canned fruits, fruit juices and vegetables, cereals and uncooked instant cereals, peanut butter, jelly, hard candy and canned nuts, Vitamin C
- **Indefinitely:** (If stored correctly) Wheat, vegetable oil, dried corn, baking powder, soybeans, instant coffee, tea and cocoa, salt, white rice, bouillon projects, dry pasta

Shopping tips

- Don't buy unfamiliar food for your stockpile. Familiar foods are comforting in a time of stress.
- Watch for items that don't need cooking, water or special preparation.
- Don't forget a manual can opener and disposable utensils.

Emergency Supplies to have ready

- Medical supplies and first aid book
- Three-day supply of food and water
- Soap, toothbrush and paste
- Portable radio, flashlights and batteries
- Shovel and other tools you think you might use
- Liquid bleach to purify drinking water.
- Money and waterproof matches
- Fire extinguisher
- Blanket and extra clothing (sleeping bag)
- Manual can opener
- Things for children and infants, if applicable

When the power goes out...

- Use perishable food and foods from the refrigerator.
- Use foods from the freezer. Foods will be safe to eat for at least three days.
- Then use non-perishable foods and staples.
- If you have snow, you can use that to keep food cold.

Stain Removal Guide

- Check the care label before you start.
- Leave non-washable fabrics to the professionals
- Test cleaning solutions on a hidden area first
- Blot the stain. Don't rub.

Grease (butter, oil, mayo) – start with combination solvent. Follow up with mineral spirits or oil solvent, if necessary.

Protein (blood, egg, grass) – soak bloodstains in cold saltwater. If necessary, flush with white vinegar or hydrogen peroxide using and eyedropper.

Fruit and vegetables (juice, jam) – Use denatured alcohol. Using an eyedropper, flush with white vinegar to remove remaining color, then dishwashing detergent to remove residue.

Red wine – Use denatured alcohol, then flush with white vinegar to get out remaining color, use a dropper. For sturdy fabric, coat area with salt, hold over the sink, and pour hot water through the fabric.

Hot drinks – Flush with lemon juice (tea) or white vinegar (coffee) to remove color, you can also use bleach. For sugar, flush with water.

Stain Removal Guide (con't)

Vinaigrette – Use a combination solvent for grease, then flush with white vinegar for color.

Wax or gum – Use ice to freeze wax or gum. Scrape or crack off as much as you can. Then use oil solvent or mineral spirits to remove residue.

Chocolate – Start with a combination solvent for grease.

Sauces (tomato, ketchup, barbecue) – Scoop off the excess. Flush with white vinegar for color.

Felt-tip ink – Flush with denatured alcohol , wash with dishwashing detergent.

Ballpoint ink – Rub glycerin into area, let stand 15 to 20 minutes; wash with dishwashing detergent. Spray with inexpensive hair spray and flush with water.

Lipstick – Use the grease solvent. Flush with white vinegar or a mild bleach to remove color.

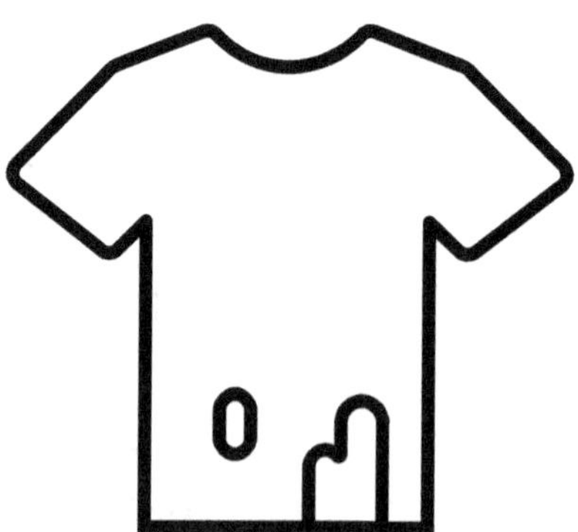

Tofu:
the underestimated food

Tofu Facts

   Tofu is soybean curd, which is a soft, cheese-like food made by curdling fresh, hot soymilk with a coagulant.

   In recipes, tofu acts like a sponge and soaks up what ever flavor it is added to. It's high is protein. It's a good source for B-vitamins and iron. It's a great source of calcium, low in sodium, and contains no cholesterol.

Three types of Tofu:

- *Firm tofu* – dense and solid. Great for stir fries, soups or on the grill. It will hold its shape.
- *Soft tofu* – Great for blending into soups or anything calling for blended tofu.
- *Silken tofu* – Creamy, custard like substance. It's great to pureed or blended dishes.

   To keep tofu fresh, keep refrigerated. To keep fresh, drain the water from the plastic tub daily and cover tofu with cold water. This is good to do for one week. If you have it longer, drain it and freeze it for up to six months.

   To thaw, pour boiling water over the tofu and let stand until pliable about five to 15 minutes. Drain and squeeze out excess water.

Helpful tips from Jackie Poch

Cook at Presque Isle County Jail, Rogers City, Michigan:

- Anything that grows under the ground, start off in cold water when cooking…potatoes, beets, carrots, etc. If it grows above ground, start off in boiling water…peas, beans, etc.
- Cut a meringue pie cleanly by lightly rubbing butter on either side of the knife
- To keep icing moist, and prevent cracking, add a pinch of baking soda to the icing.

Recipe : Barbequed Tofu

Ingredients:

1 lb. firm tofu that has been frozen
and defrosted
1 c. barbecue sauce
2 large onions, thinly sliced

Cooking Instructions :

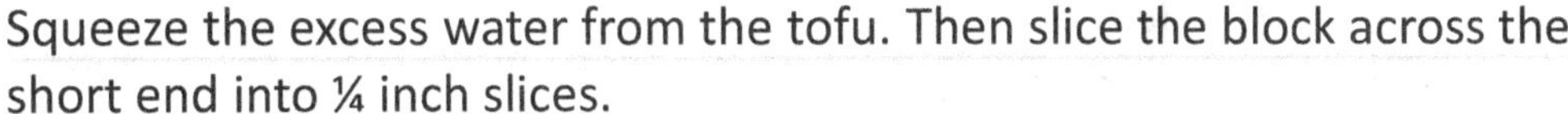

Squeeze the excess water from the tofu. Then slice the block across the short end into ¼ inch slices.
Place the sliced onions in baking dish and pour ¼ c. of barbecue sauce over them.
Add the tofu and remaining barbecue sauce.
Let marinate in sauce, refrigerated, for several hours.
Bake at 375 degrees for 20 to 30 minutes until the sauce is bubbly and hot.

Notes :

Tofu can be grilled , brushing frequently with barbecue sauce.

Recipe provided by the Soyfoods Association of America

Recipe : Tofu Pumpkin Pie

DIFFICULTY:

RATING:

PREP TIME:

COOK TIME:

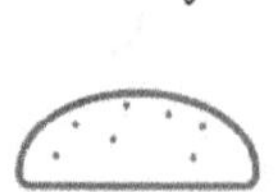

Ingredients:

10 oz. soft, silken tofu, blended in
a blender until smooth
1 – 16 oz. can pumpkin
¾ c. sugar
2 tsp. salt
1 tsp. ground cinnamon

½ tsp. ground ginger
¼ tsp. ground cloves
1 – 9: unbaked pie shell

Cooking Instructions :

Pre-heat oven to 425 degrees
Cream together the pumpkin and sugar.
Add the salt, spices and blended tofu, mixing until thoroughly blended together.
Pour into pie shell.
Bake at 425 for 15 minutes.
Lower the heat to 350 degrees and bake for an additional 40 minutes

Notes :

Recipe provided by the Soyfoods Association of America

Recipe : Tofu South of the Border Enchiladas

DIFFICULTY:

RATING:

PREP TIME:

COOK TIME:

Ingredients:

8 – 8" whole wheat tortillas
½ c. chopped onion
3/ c. chopped sweet green pepper
1 – 4 oz. can chopped mild green chilies
1 clove garlic
½ tsp. cumin seed

1 tsp. dried cilantro
12 oz. silken firm tofu, drained and mashed
2 c. diced tomatoes, drained
2 c. thick tomato salsa
½ c. low fat cheddar cheese, shredded

Cooking Instructions :

Preheat oven to 350 degrees. Spray a 9" x 13" baking pan.
In bowl, combine all ingredients except tortillas, tomato, salsa and cheese.
Place ½ c. of mixture in center of each tortilla and roll. Place in baking dish, seam side down.
Pour salsa over enchiladas. Sprinkle with cheese. Cover pan with aluminum foil and bake for 25 to 30 minutes.

Notes :

Serves 8.

Recipe provided by the Soyfoods Association of America

Beverages

Recipe : Hot Cranberry Punch

DIFFICULTY:

RATING:

PREP TIME:

COOK TIME:

Ingredients:

1 qt. cranberry juice cocktail
2 c. orange juice
1 c. lemon juice
1/3 c. honey
3 whole cloves
2 sticks of cinnamon

1 qt. ginger ale

Cooking Instructions :

- Mix altogether into a 3=quart saucepan
- Simmer 15 min. Remove spices.
- Add 1 qt. ginger ale just before serving. Garnish with fresh cranberries.
- Serve hot it cups or punch bowl.

Notes :

From the mess hall of Niola Giffin. Submitted by Alola G. Morrison, Army Reserve and Public Health

Recipe : Mint Punch

DIFFICULTY:

RATING:

PREP TIME:

COOK TIME:

Ingredients:

1 c. sugar
2 c. water, hot
1 c. crushed mint leaves
Juice of six lemons
1 qt. ginger ale

Cooking Instructions :

- Make a syrup of the sugar and hot water.
- Add crushed mint leaves to the hot water/sugar mix and let "stand" until cool. Strain.
- Add the juice of 6 lemons.
- Use 1/3 glass of this mint syrup with ice and fill with ginger ale for each person.
- Stir and serve immediately.
- May add a sprig of mint in each glass as it is being served.

Notes :

From the mess hall of Alola G. Morrison
Army Reserve and US Public Health

Recipe : Raspberry Punch

DIFFICULTY:

RATING:

PREP TIME:

COOK TIME:

Ingredients:

1 Pint Hognindof Raspberry Sherbet (or your favorite kind)
2 liter regular Sprite or diet Sprite
Fresh or frozen raspberries

Cooking Instructions :

Add sherbet and sprite to your favorite punch bowl, then put in the fruit for a chill non-alcoholic beverage.

Notes :

From the mess hall of Diana Greenier.

Recipe : Slush

Ingredients:

1 ¼ C. sugar
2 c. boiling water
3 c. cold water (after hot water
and sugar is dissolved)
6 oz. concentrated orange juice
6 oz. lemonade

2 c. strong tea
2 c. Bourbon or blend

Cooking Instructions :

- Mix altogether and place in a bowl to freeze.
- Bring out this frozen mix ½ hour before serving. Mix in a food processor to get the "slush" affect.

Notes :

From the mess hall of Niola Giffin. Submitted by Alola G. Morrison, Army Reserve and Public Health

Breakfast

Recipe : Baked Oatmeal

DIFFICULTY:

RATING:

PREP TIME:

COOK TIME:

Ingredients:

½ c. oil (Canola)
2 eggs beaten
1/3 c. sugar
3 c. Old Fashioned Oats
2 tsp. baking powder
1 c. milk
Raisins, nuts, cinnamon

Cooking Instructions :

Mix oil, eggs, sugar. Add the rest and mix well.
Pour into baking dish.
Cook at 350 for 30 to 35 minutes

Notes :

Makes 6 to 8 servings

From the mess hall of Shirley Merrill.

Recipe : Doughnut Muffins

Ingredients:

1 egg
1/3 c. cooking oil
½ c. milk
1 ½ c. flour
½ c. sugar
2 tsp. baking powder
½ tsp. vanilla

Cooking Instructions :

Dot with butter.
Sprinkle cinnamon and sugar.

Bake at 400 for 15 minutes.

Notes :

From the mess hall of Nina Braley.

Recipe : Quiche

DIFFICULTY:

RATING:

PREP TIME:

COOK TIME:

Ingredients:

28 finely crushed saltines
4 to 5 Tbsp. melted butter
2 beaten eggs
8 oz. shredded swiss cheese
(Jarlsberg or Gruyere)
¾ c. sour cream
1 C. sauteed onion

Dash pepper
1 ½ c. raw vegetables -
Zucchini slices, broccoli,
Mushrooms, fresh spinach.

Cooking Instructions :

Combine saltines with butter and press into 9 in. pie plate.
In mixing bowl, combine eggs, swiss cheese, sour cream, onion and dash
of pepper. Then add raw veggies.
Pour mixture into cracker shell and top with grated parmesan cheese.
Bake at 375 for 30 minutes. Let sit 15 minutes before cutting.

Notes :

Try broccoli and mushrooms with 3 or 4 slices of cooked
crumbled bacon.

From the mess hall of Charlene Gilman.

Recipe : Smoked Sausage Casserole

DIFFICULTY:

RATING:

PREP TIME:

COOK TIME:

Ingredients:

1 pkg. cut up or sliced
4 to 6 carrots cut up
4 to 6 potatoes
Top with 2 tsp. butter
½ tsp. oregano
1 tsp. basil
Cover with drizzle of olive oil

Cooking Instructions :

In a foiled pan, add all ingredients, cook in 375 oven for 40 to 45 minutes.

Notes :

Serves 6

From the mess hall of Nina Fraley.

Recipe : Vets Frittata

DIFFICULTY:

RATING:

PREP TIME:

COOK TIME:

Ingredients:

Olive oil
3 eggs
¾ c. egg whites
1 Tbsp milk
Salt, pepper, basil, oregano

¼ lb. ground sausage
½ c. shredded cheese

Cooking Instructions :

Sauté in 3 tablespoons of olive oil: ¼ pound ground sausage (or anything you'd like instead)
Beat until foamy: 3 eggs, ¾ c egg whites, 1 tablespoon each of milk and water.
Add salt, pepper, basil, oregano to your liking.
Add ½ cup shredded cheese and the sautéed sausage to the egg mixture.
Cook (no stirring) with 2 tablespoons olive oil in a round skillet on medium heat about 5 minutes then flip into another round skillet to   cook other side about 5 minutes.

Notes :

- Serves 2 – Serve on plate – top with a mixture of 1/8 c. lemon juice, 1/8 c. olive oil, 1 c. cut up arugula, ½ c. diced tomato, 1 cut up avocado, small can sliced olives.

From the mess hall of Rachel Akins.

Appetizers

Recipe : 9 Day Pickles

DIFFICULTY:

RATING:

PREP TIME:

COOK TIME:

Ingredients:

7 lbs. small cucumbers
salt water that will float an egg
vinegar
1 tsp. powdered alum

<u>Syrup</u> for day 7:
6 c. sugar and 3 pints vinegar
brought to a boil

½ dozen sticks of cinnamon
½ dozen cloves

Cooking Instructions :

For 3 days soak 7 lbs. of small, whole cucumbers in salt water.
<u>Day 4</u>: Cut off stems and split cucumbers lengthwise into quarters or slice.
Soak them in fresh water for 3 more days.
<u>Day 7</u>: Place cucumbers in a weak solution of vinegar and water and 1 tsp.
of powdered alum.
Heat 1 ½ hours. DO NOT BOIL.
Drain. Add the <u>syrup</u>, sticks of cinnamon and cloves.
Let sit for 2 days more.
Jar and seal.

Notes :

From the mess hall of Pat Salmon.

Recipe : Chinese Chicken Wings

DIFFICULTY:

RATING:

PREP TIME:

COOK TIME:

Ingredients:

5 oz. soy sauce
1/3 c. brown sugar
1 tbsp. ginger
1 tbsp. minced garlic
½ lbs. chicken wings

Cooking Instructions :

Mix all together and marinate overnight.
Cook at 425 for 30 to 40 minutes.

Notes :

You can double the recipe for larger groups.

From the mess hall of Nina Braley.

Recipe : Crabmeat Dip

DIFFICULTY:

RATING:

PREP TIME:

COOK TIME:

Ingredients:

1 lg. can Crabmeat (or fresh)
1 can Snow's minced clams, drained
1 - 8oz. pkg. Cream cheese
1/3 c. Miracle Whip
1/8 stick of butter
Garlic salt
Accent (Seasoned Salt)

Cooking Instructions :

Melt butter, cream cheese, Miracle Whip in double boiler
just until blended. It will curdle if it gets too hot.
Add rest of Ingredients. Make the day before for best flavor.
Reheat in double boiler.
Serve in fondu with crackers or toast rounds.

Notes :

No substitutes. Use real ingredients. (Cream cheese,
butter, Miracle Whip)

From the mess hall of Shirley Merrill.

Recipe : English Muffin Appetizers

DIFFICULTY:

RATING:

PREP TIME:

COOK TIME:

Ingredients:

1 jar Old English Cheese Spread
½ stick butter
¼ tsp. garlic powder
½ tsp. salt
1 Tbsp. mayonnaise
1 can shrimp or crabmeat

One package of English muffins
Optional: Red pepper

Cooking Instructions :

Mix all of the ingredients together.
Spread on English muffins
Broil until bubbly.
Cut into quarters. Enjoy!

Notes :

From the mess hall of Shirley Merrill.

Recipe : Hot Pizza Dip

DIFFICULTY:

RATING:

PREP TIME:

COOK TIME:

Ingredients:

1 pkg. (8 oz.) cream cheese
1 tsp. Italian seasoning
¼ tsp. garlic powder
2 c. shredded mozzarella cheese
1 c. shredded cheddar cheese
½ c. pizza sauce

1/1 c. finely chopped
green pepper
Tortilla chips or breadsticks

Cooking Instructions :

In a bowl, combine cream cheese, Italian seasoning and garlic powder.
Spread on the bottom of a greased 9- inch pie plate. Combine the cheeses;
sprinkle half over the cream cheese layer.
Top with the pizza sauce and peppers. Sprinkle with the remaining cheeses.
Bake at 350 for 20 minutes.
Serve warm with tortilla chips or breadsticks.

Notes :

Makes about 3 ½ cups.

From the mess hall of Celeste Kennedy.

Recipe : Meatballs

Ingredients:

1 lb. lean hamburger
1 c. breadcrumbs (seasoned)
½ c. grated parmesan cheese
1 tsp. parsley
1 clove garlic or ½ tsp. garlic salt
½ c. milk

2 eggs beaten
Salt and pepper to taste

Cooking Instructions :

Combine everything and mix and make balls and brown in oven
on cookie sheet (Can use broiler pan – so fat will drain)
Add to sauce and heat.
Cook in oven for 20 min. at 375. Makes 25 – ¾ inch balls.

Notes :

Can be used for spaghetti and meatballs or with mushroom and
onion sauce and gravy.

From the mess hall of one of our Veteran friends.

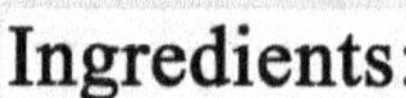

DIFFICULTY:

RATING:

PREP TIME:

COOK TIME: 15 to 20 min

Ingredients:

8 oz. mushrooms
1 slice break or breadcrumbs
1 small onion chopped
Dash of garlic powder
Dash of pepper
1 Tbsp. butter

Opt. 2 tsp. white wine (or 2 Tbsp. Soy sauce)

Cooking Instructions :

Stem mushrooms. Cut stems into small pieces. Add to onion and
Butter. Add garlic and pepper.
Sauté for 2 minutes. Add bread and soy sauce.
Stuff mushrooms.
You can also pour a little soy sauce over the mushrooms
before baking.
Bake 15 to 20 minutes at 350.

Notes :

From the mess hall of one of our Veteran friends.

Salads and soups

Recipe : 3 Bean Salad

DIFFICULTY:

RATING:

PREP TIME:

COOK TIME:

Ingredients:

16 oz green beans cut
16 oz yellow wax beans cut
16 oz kidney beans – dark red
½ c. green or red pepper diced
½ c. celery – diced
½ c. onion finely chopped

Dressing:
2/3 c. distilled vinegar
2/3 c. sugar or Splenda
1/3 c. salad oil
1 tsp. salt
½ tsp. pepper

Cooking Instructions :

Rinse all beans thoroughly. Mix all above in large steel bowl.

Dressing: Dissolve sugar in vinegar. Then mix remaining
Ingredients. Pour over beans. Mix well.
Cover and refrigerate until ready to serve.

Notes :

From the mess hall of Jerry Black

Recipe : Crock-Pot Beef Stew

DIFFICULTY:

RATING:

PREP TIME:

COOK TIME:

5-7 hours

Ingredients:

4 lbs. stew beef
4 Tbsp. margarine or salt pork fat
Flour to dredge beef
2 Tbsp. salt
½ tsp. pepper
8 c. hot water
½ c. catsup

2 bay leaves
4 large onions, peeled, and quartered or sliced
12 carrots, pared and quartered
8 medium potatoes, pared and quartered
2 c. diced celery

Cooking Instructions :

Cut beef into 1-inch cubes. Put flour, salt and pepper into a paper bag. Shake up beef in bag.
Melt fat in heavy pan with tight fitting cover. Brown beef in melted fat.
Put into a crock-pot. Add sliced onions, celery, catsup, bay leaves and hot water. Cook on low 5-7 hours.
Mix about 1/3 c. flour with 2/3 c. cold water, allow to set; then when stew is ready, add flour mixture to thicken.

Notes :

From the mess hall of Jerry Black.

Recipe : Fruit Salad

DIFFICULTY:

RATING:

PREP TIME:

COOK TIME:

Ingredients:

½ lb. mini marshmallows
1 med. can pineapple chunks
drained (save juice)
¾ c. pecans
Pinch of salt

Dressing: 1 tbsp. rounded flour
1 tbsp. sugar, 1 tsp. butter
Pinch salt
Juice from ½ med. lemon and juice from
pineapple
1 lg. egg, beaten (separated from
everything.)

Cooking Instructions :

In a saucepan, mix flour, sugar, salt, lemon and pineapple juice.
Cook slowly on low temp until clear and somewhat thicker.
Add small amount of hot liquid into beaten egg in a small bowl mixing all
the time. Add more liquid little by little until you have 1/3 c. hot mix to
pour into rest of hot thickened liquid.
Cook until thick. Pour over a bowl of marshmallows and mix.
Cool and serve. Cover with whipped cream.

Notes :

From the mess hall of Annette Morrison, Alola Morrison's mother-in-
law.

Recipe : Flouffy Salad

DIFFICULTY:

RATING:

PREP TIME:

COOK TIME:

Ingredients:

20 oz. or larger can of fruit cocktail with most of the juice
3 oz. pkg. instant (sugar free) pistachio pudding mix
8 oz. frozen (sugar free) whipped topping thawed

Cooking Instructions :

Combine fruit and dry pudding mix.
Fold in whipped topping.
Refrigerate.

Notes :

Recipe from the mess hall of twins Auntie June & Jeanette (Mom).

Submitted by Nancy June Cobb.

Recipe : Irish Stew

DIFFICULTY:

RATING:

PREP TIME:

COOK TIME: 10-12 hours

Ingredients:

2 lbs. boneless beef, cubed, browned and drained
2 tsp. salt
¼ tsp. pepper
2 c. water
1 small whole bay leaf

2 medium carrots, pared and cut in ½ inch slices
2 small onions, thinly sliced
3 to 4 medium potatoes, pared and quartered
¼ c quick-cooking tapioca (opt.)
1 10oz. frozen peas of mixed veg.

Cooking Instructions :

Season cubed beef with salt and pepper. Add remaining ingredients except peas (omit tapioca if you don't want gravy thickened).
Stir well. Cover and cook on Low 10-12 hours. Add peas during last 1 to 2 hours of cooking.

Bread/crackers goes well with this stew.

Notes :

From the mess hall of Jerry Black.

Recipe : Grape Salad

DIFFICULTY:

RATING:

PREP TIME:

COOK TIME:

Ingredients:

1 ½ lbs. green grapes
1 ½ lbs. red grapes
8 oz. cream cheese
1 c. sour cream
½ c. sugar
1 tsp. vanilla

Cooking Instructions :

Wash and dry grapes.
Put grapes in a 9x12 pan.
Put all other ingredients in bowl. Mix well with mixer.
Spoon onto grapes and mix
Mix: ½ c. brown sugar and ½ c. nuts. Sprinkle over top and
chill overnight.

Notes :

From the mess hall of Pam Whynot.

Recipe : Macaroni & Cheese Salad

Ingredients:

1 c. Macaroni, cooked, drained-cooled
1 - 12oz. can ham, cut in strips
1 c. Cheddar cheese, cubed or shredded
½ c celery chopped

1/3 c. green pepper, chopped
2 Tbsp. Pimento chopped
¼ c. Pickle relish, drained
½ c. Salad dressing
1 Tbsp. prepared mustard
¼ tsp. salt

Cooking Instructions :

Blend first 8 ingredients then toss others lightly and chill.

Notes :

From the mess hall of Jerry Black.

Recipe : Pear-Lime Gelatin Salad

DIFFICULTY:

RATING:

PREP TIME:

COOK TIME:

Ingredients:

1 can (15oz) pear halves
1 pkg. (3 oz.) lime gelatin
1 pkg (8oz) cream cheese-cubed
1 can (20 oz) crushed pineapple
1 c. chopped pecans – toasted/divided
1 carton whipped topping

Cooking Instructions :

Drain pears and reserve juice. In a small sauce pan, bring juice
to a boil. Stir in gelatin until dissolved. Cool slightly.
In food processor, combine pear and cream cheese. Process until
smooth. Transfer to large bowl. Stir in gelatin mixture until blended.
Stir in pineapple and ¾ c. pecans. Fold in whipped topping.
Pour in ungreased dish.
Sprinkle remaining pecans on top. Refrigerate until set.
Use a 11x7x2 pan.

Notes :

You can use any pan as long as it will hold everything.

From the mess hall of Shirley Merrill.

Recipe : Sweet n Sour Sauce

DIFFICULTY:

RATING:

PREP TIME:

COOK TIME:

Ingredients:

½ c. packed brown sugar
1 Tbsp. cornstarch
1/3 c. vinegar
1 Tbsp. soy sauce
13 ¼ oz. can pineapple chunks
1 sm. Green pepper coarsely chopped.
Your choice of meat

Cooking Instructions :

Mix brown sugar and cornstarch in skillet. Stir in pineapple
with juice, vinegar and soy sauce.
Heat to boiling stirring constantly.
Add meat.
Cover and simmer 10 minutes. Stir in green pepper.
Cover, simmer 5 more minutes.

Notes :

From one of our Veteran friends.

Recipe : Wilted Lettuce Salad

DIFFICULTY:

RATING:

PREP TIME:

COOK TIME:

Ingredients:

1 med. Head iceberg lettuce
4 to 6 slices bacon, cook until
crisp (save fat)
2 tbsp. sugar
¼ tsp. salt
½ tsp. black pepper

2 lg. eggs
2 Tbsp. white vinegar
1 med. onion cut up fine

Cooking Instructions :

Cook eggs over hard, then chop fine.
Break up lettuce leave. Rinse in cold water and drain extra water from
the leaves. Pat with clean dish towel to get the lettuce dry as possible.
Put lettuce in a large mixing bowl and sprinkle with sugar, salt, pepper
and onion. Crumple the bacon over all. Add cooked chopped eggs. Mix.
Stir in hot bacon fat over the lettuce. Heat the vinegar and add to mix.
Serve immediately.

Notes :

From the mess hall of Annette Morrison, Alola Morrison's mother-in-law.

Recipe : Winter Salad

DIFFICULTY:

RATING:

PREP TIME:

COOK TIME:

Ingredients:

1 c. sour cream
1 c. small marshmallows
2 Tbsp. cut up maraschino cherries
1 c. canned crushed drained pineapples
1 c. mandarin oranges drained

Cooking Instructions :

Mix altogether in a medium bowl and refrigerate.
Serve cold.

Notes :

From the mess hall of Alola G. Morrison, Army Reserve and Public Health

Breads

Recipe : Apple-Cranberry Muffins

DIFFICULTY:

RATING:

PREP TIME:

COOK TIME: 20-25 minutes

Ingredients:

1 ¾ c. + 2 Tbsp. all-purpose flour
½ c. sugar, divided
1 ½ Tbsp. baking powder
½ tsp. salt
½ tsp. baking soda
1 egg

¾ c. milk
¾ c. sweetened applesauce
¼ c. butter, melted
1 c. fresh cranberries, coarsely chopped
½ tsp. ground cinnamon

Cooking Instructions :

In medium bowl, combine 1 ¾ cups flour, ¼ cup sugar, baking
Powder, baking soda, and salt. In small bowl, combine egg, milk, applesauce, and
butter; mix well. Add egg mix to flour mix. Stir just until moistened. Batter will be
lumpy. Do not overmix. In small bowl, toss cranberries with remaining 2
tablespoons of flour. Fold into
batter. Spoon batter into 12 greased 2 ¾ inch muffin cups.
In measuring cup, combine remaining ¼ cup of sugar and cinnamon.
Sprinkle over tops of muffins. Bake in preheated 400° oven for
20-25 minutes or golden brown.

Notes :

From the mess hall of Jerry Black.

Recipe : Banana Bread

DIFFICULTY:

RATING:

PREP TIME:

COOK TIME: 45 to 60 min.

Ingredients:

2 ½ c. flour
1 c. sugar
3 ½ tsp. baking powder
2 or 3 bananas
¾ c. milk
3 Tbsp. cooking oil
1 egg

Cooking Instructions :

Put all ingredients in one bowl.
Mix 30 seconds until all is incorporated.
Bake at 350 for 60 minutes.

Notes :

From the mess hall of Shirley Merrill.

<table>
<tr><td>

Recipe : Banana Bread

</td><td>

DIFFICULTY:

RATING:

PREP TIME:

COOK TIME: 1 hour

</td><td>

</td></tr>
</table>

Ingredients:

1/3 c. shortening
2/3 c. sugar
2 eggs
1 ¾ c. flour

2 tsp. baking powder
¼ tsp. soda
1 c. mashed ripe banana
½ c. chopped walnuts

Cooking Instructions :

Cream sugar and shortening. Add eggs, one at a time, beating
after each egg is added.
Sift dry ingredients together and stir into the creamed mixture.
Blend in the mashed banana. Stir in the chopped nuts.
Pour into a greased loaf pan and bake in a 350° oven for 1 hour
or until a tester comes out clean. Remove from oven.
Let rest 10 minutes and then turn out onto a rack to cool.

Notes :

From the mess hall of Jerry Black.

Recipe : Banana Nut Bread

DIFFICULTY:

RATING:

PREP TIME:

COOK TIME: 1 hour

Ingredients:

½ c. shortening
1 c. brown sugar
2 egg
2 mashed bananas
½ chopped nuts (walnuts)

2 c. flour
1 tsp. baking soda
½ salt

Cooking Instructions :

Cream shortening – add sugar gradually and cream well.
Add eggs one at a time.
Add mashed bananas, nuts and sifted dry ingredients.
Pour into a greased bread pan.

Bake 1 hour at 350°.

Notes :

From the mess hall of Pat Salmon.

Recipe : Banana Tea Bread

DIFFICULTY:

RATING:

PREP TIME:

COOK TIME:

Ingredients:

1 ¾ c. sifted all purpose flour
2 tsp. baking powder
¼ tsp. baking soda
½ tsp. salt
1/3 c. shortening
2/3 c. sugar

2 lg. eggs, unbeaten
1 c. mashed ripe bananas (about 2)
½ c. finely chopped nuts (walnuts)

Cooking Instructions :

Preheat oven to 350 degrees.
Grease and dust loaf pan.
Mix flour baking powder, salt and soda and set aside.
Cream thoroughly shortening and sugar.
Add eggs to sugar and shortening until light and fluffy.
Blend in flour mix until smooth.
Turn into loaf pan. Cook for 1 hour. Cool for 10 min. before cutting.

Notes :

From the mess hall of Alola G. Morrison, Army Reserve and Public Health

Recipe : Biscuit Supreme

DIFFICULTY:

RATING:

PREP TIME:

COOK TIME:

Ingredients:

2 c. sifted all purpose flour
4 tsp. baking powder
½ tsp. salt
½ tsp. cream of tartar
2 tsp. sugar

½ c. shortening
2/3 c. milk

Cooking Instructions :

Sift together flour, baking powder, salt, cream of tartar and
sugar.
Cut in shortening, until mixture is coarse and crumbles.
Add milk all at once. Stir until dough rolls around.
Kneed ½ minute.
Roll or pat dough to ½ thickness.
Bake on ungreased baking sheet at 450 for 10 to 12 minutes.

Notes :

From the mess hall of Roma Shaw. Her husband was
an engineman in the Navy. He loved these biscuits with a soup.

Recipe : Blueberry Muffins

DIFFICULTY:

RATING:

PREP TIME:

COOK TIME: 35 minutes

Ingredients:

2 ½ c. sifted flour
2 ½ tsp. baking powder
1/3 c. sugar
½ tsp. salt
1 egg yolk slightly beaten
1 c. milk

4 Tbsp. margarine
1 egg white stiffly beaten
1 c. blueberries

Cooking Instructions :

Sift flour once, add baking powder, sugar and salt; sift again.
Combine egg yolk and milk. Add to flour mixture.
Add shortening – then mix only enough to dampen flour.
Fold in egg white and blueberries.
Bake in greased muffin pans in hot oven at 425° for 25 minutes.

Makes 12.

Notes :

From the mess hall of Shirley Merrill.

Recipe : Easy Biscuits

Ingredients:

4 c. flour
4 tsp. bakewell cream
2 tsp. baking soda
1 tsp. salt
½ c. mayonnaise
1 ¾ c. cold milk

Cooking Instructions :

Mix. Roll out flour onto floured surface to ½ to ¾ inch thick.
Cook at 475 for 5 minutes. Shut off oven and cook on stored heat
for 10 to 15 minutes until golden brown.

Notes :

From the mess hall of Nina Braley.

Recipe : Honey-Oatmeal Bread

DIFFICULTY:

RATING:

PREP TIME:

COOK TIME: 50 minutes

Ingredients:

1 ½ c. rolled oats (quick cooking, not instant)
1/3 c. honey
¼ c. butter or margarine
1 Tbsp. salt

1 c. sour cream
2 pkg. active dry yeast
2 eggs
4 ½ c. all-purpose flour
¼ lb. honey butter

Cooking Instructions :

Combine 1 cup boiling water and first 4 ingredients and stir until butter is melted. Add sour cream and cool to lukewarm. Soften yeast in ½ cup of warm water. Add yeast, eggs, and 2 cups flour to oat mixture and beat until smooth. Add enough more flour to make a stiff dough. Turn onto lightly floured board and knead until elastic. Cover dough on board with towel or in a bowl and let rest 20 minutes. Divide in 2 equal portions and shape into 2 loaves. Put each into a greased 9x5x3 inch loaf pan. Cover pans loosely with plastic Wrap and refrigerate 12 to 24 hours. When ready to bake, let stand at room temp 10 minutes. Bake at 375° for 50 minutes or when done.

Notes :

From the mess hall of Mom Moody's files

Recipe : Irish Soda Bread

DIFFICULTY:

RATING:

PREP TIME:

COOK TIME: 1 hour

Ingredients:

4 c. flour
4 tsp. baking powder
½ c. sugar
1 tsp. salt
1 Tbsp. Crisco
1 - 13oz. box of seedless raisins or currants

2 Tbsp. caraway seeds
1 egg
½ c. milk

Cooking Instructions :

Rinse raisins in colander under warm water to soften.
Put first 4 ingredients in a bowl.
Add Crisco, raisins and caraway.
In second bowl, beat egg with milk.
Make hole in dry ingredients. Pour egg mixture in hole. Continue mixing until well mixed – batter will be stiff.
Pour in 9" cake pan.
Make a cross on top.
Bake 10 mins at 410° then reduce heat to 350° for 50 minutes.
Remove from oven & cover top with melted butter.

Notes :

From the mess hall of Betty O'Brien

Recipe : Pumpkin Bread

DIFFICULTY:

RATING:

PREP TIME:

COOK TIME:

Ingredients:

1 can pumpkin (2 cups)
4 eggs
1 c. oil
2/3 c. cold water
3 c. sugar
3 1/3 c. flour

2 tsp. soda
1 ½ tsp. cinnamon
1 tsp. nutmeg
Pecans (optional)

Cooking Instructions :

Sift dry ingredients together. Beat egg until thick.
Add pumpkin, oil, water.
Add this to dry ingredients. Beat with electric mixer to mix well.
Bake for 1 hour at 350.

Notes :

Makes three small loaves.

From the mess hall of Shirley Merrill.

Recipe : Pumpkin Bars

DIFFICULTY:

RATING:

PREP TIME:

COOK TIME:

Ingredients:

4 eggs
2 c. sugar
1 – 15 oz. can pumpkin
2 tsp. baking powder
1 tsp. baking soda
2 c. Gluten free all-purpose flour

1 tsp. ginger
2 tsp. cinnamon
½ tsp. nutmeg
¾ tsp. salt

Cooking Instructions :

Mix all together.
Bake at 350 for 35 to 40 minutes in a 9x12 pan.

Notes :

From the mess hall of Nina Braley.

Recipe : Raised angel biscuits

DIFFICULTY:

RATING:

PREP TIME:

COOK TIME:

Ingredients:

1 env. yeast
¼ c. warm water
2 ½ c. flour
½ tsp. baking soda
1 c. buttermilk
1 tsp. baking powder

1 tsp. salt
1/8 c. sugar
½ c. Crisco shortening

Cooking Instructions :

Put yeast in ¼ c. warm water and set aside after everything is done.
Mix yeast and water.
Mix dry items in order given.
Cut in shortening. Stir in buttermilk and water/yeast mixture.
Blend well.
Put on flour board – kneed, roll out and cut. Put in greased pan.
Let sit until raised to double size. (About 1 ½ hour or so.)
Bake at 400 for 10 minutes.

Notes :

From the mess hall of Shirley Merrill.

Ingredients:

1 ½ c. brown sugar
2/3 c. oil
2eggs
1 tsp. salt
1 tsp. vanilla
2 tsps. Cinnamon
1 c. buttermilk

1 tsp. baking soda
2 ½ c. four
1 ½ to 2 c. rhubarb, chopped
¾ c. chopped nuts
Topping: ½ c. brown sugar,
¼ c. butter

Cooking Instructions :

Beat together the brown sugar, oil and eggs. Add the salt, vanilla
and cinnamon. Add the buttermilk and baking soda.
Then, add the flour, rhubarb and nuts.
Sprinkle with topping. Bake at 350 in two loaf pans for 1 hour.

For Topping: Mix brown sugar, but in butter, flour and
1/3 c. chopped nuts.

Notes :

From the mess hall of Shirley Merrill.

Recipe : Sour Cream Cranberry Bread

DIFFICULTY:

RATING:

PREP TIME:

COOK TIME:

Ingredients:

2 c. flour
1 tsp. baking powder
¼ tsp. baking soda
½ c. butter
1 c. sugar
½ tsp. almond extract

2 eggs
8 oz. sour cream or cream cheese
1 can whole berry cranberry sauce
½ c. nuts

Cooking Instructions :

In bowl, sift together flour, baking powder and baking soda.
Add butter, extract, eggs, cream cheese.
In buttered 10x10x2 pan, add ½ batter then ½ cranberry sauce,
then repeat, ending with batter.
Bake at 350 for 40 to 45 minutes.
Let cool for 10 minutes.

Notes :

From the mess hall of Shirley Merrill.

Recipe : Streusel Coffeecake

Ingredients:

¾ c. sugar
1/3 c. Crisco oil
1 egg
½ c. milk
1 ½ c. sifted regular flour
2 tsp. double-acting baking power
½ tsp. salt

Streusel Topping
½ c. light brown sugar
2 T regular flour
2 tsp. cinnamon
2 T Crisco oil
½ c. finely-chopped walnuts
(combined with a fork)

Cooking Instructions :

Combine sugar, Crisco oil and egg.
Add milk and beat thoroughly.
Stir combined dry ingredients. Beat until smooth.
Spread in a greased 9-inch square pan.
Sprinkle with Streusel Topping.
Bake at 375° for 30-35 minutes.

Notes :

From the mess hall of one of our Veteran friends.

Recipe : Zoom Pretzels

DIFFICULTY:

RATING:

PREP TIME:

COOK TIME: 5-10 minutes

Ingredients:

1 small package of yeast
4 c. flour
1 ½ c. water
1 Tbsp. sugar

Cooking Instructions :

Mix all the above together.
Knead well on floured surface.
Make into shapes, i.e. braids, balls, pretzel shapes, etc.
Rub the top of shape with a beaten egg, add salt.
Bake on an ungreased sheet at 450°.

Yield approx. 40 pretzels.
Bake 5-10 minutes until golden brown.

Notes :

From the mess hall of one of our Veteran friends.

Recipe : Zucchini Bread

DIFFICULTY:

RATING:

PREP TIME:

COOK TIME:

Ingredients:

Blend:
2 c. Sugar
1 c. Oil
3 tsp. Vanilla
3 Well beaten eggs
Stir in: 2 c. raw zucchini

Sift together:
2 c. Flour
¼ tsp. Baking powder
2 tsp. Baking soda
1 tsp. Salt
3 tsp. Cinnamon
½ tsp. Nutmeg

Cooking Instructions :

Combine two mixtures. Fold in 1 cup of chopped nuts.
Pour in two floured and greased pans 9x5.
Cook at 350 degrees for 1 hour.

Notes :

From the mess hall of Shirley Merrill.

Side dishes

Recipe : Asparagus Luncheon Sauce

Ingredients:

2 lb. asparagus
1 - 10oz. can cream mushroom soup
½ c. light cream
1 Tbsp. lemon juice
1 egg yolk

Cooking Instructions :

Boil asparagus about 10 minutes.
Mix above ingredients and heat slowly until it bubbles.
Drain the asparagus. Layer asparagus on toast with sauce.
Serves 6 to 8.

Notes :

From the mess hall of Jerry Black.

Recipe : Butternut Squash Casserole

DIFFICULTY:

RATING:

PREP TIME:

COOK TIME:

Ingredients:

1 pkg. of cut up butternut squash
¼ c. margarine/butter
3 Tbsp. brown sugar
¼ tsp. cinnamon rounded
¼ tsp. nutmeg rounded
¾ tsp. salt
2 large apples, cut up

Cooking Instructions :

Melt margarine, brown sugar and condiments and hold aside.
Cut up squash and apple and place in a greased casserole dish.
Pour heated mixture over top of apples and squash.
Bake at 350 degrees for 50 minutes covered.

Serves 6 to 8

Notes :

You can substitute 1 ½ Tbsp. brown sugar and 1 ½ Tbsp. Splenda for the 3 Tbsp. brown sugar.

From the mess hall of Alola G. Morrison, Army Reserve and Public Health.

Recipe : Cabbage Rolls

DIFFICULTY:

RATING:

PREP TIME:

COOK TIME:

Ingredients:

1 ½ - 2 lbs. ground beef
¾ c. rice
2 med. Onions
4-6 ribs of celery
Salt/pepper to taste
1 egg

1 can kraut
1 can of tomatoes

Cooking Instructions :

Beat 1 egg and roughly mix all ingredients together in bottom of baking dishes.
Put can of kraut on top with tomatoes.
Place cabbage core side down in water to boil until transparent and pliable.
Cut leaves off core and put aside. Put cabbage back on the stove.
Roll baking dish mixture into balls, then wrap with cabbage.
Bake for an hour at 350 to 375 degrees.

Notes :

Make them small and use a toothpick as an appetizer.

From the mess hall of Celeste Kennedy.

Recipe : Carrot Casserole

DIFFICULTY:

RATING:

PREP TIME:

COOK TIME:

Ingredients:

8 to 10 large carrots, diced,
but not too small. Cook until
tender. Drain.
¼ c. brown sugar
1 c. half and half, or cream
1 c. grated cheddar cheese
¼ c. onion diced.

Cooking Instructions :

Mix the five ingredients together. Put in large casserole dish.
Top with 1 stack Ritz crackers crushed. Mixed with one stick butter.

Bake at 350 until hot.

Notes :

From the mess hall of Edith Patterson. Submitted by Shirley Merrill.

Recipe : Crockpot Macaroni and Cheese

DIFFICULTY:

RATING:

PREP TIME:

COOK TIME:

Ingredients:

1 lb. macaroni (al dante) 16 oz. (can us gluten free pasta)
1 small Velveeta block cheese cut up
1 stick of butter (cut up)
2 – 16 oz. cans evaporated milk

Cooking Instructions :

Mix together in crockpot low for 2 ½ hours.
Stir a few times during cooking.

Notes :

From the mess hall of Nina Braley.

Recipe : Ginger, Glazed Carrots

DIFFICULTY:

RATING:

PREP TIME:

COOK TIME:

Ingredients:

1 to 2 cups small carrots, whole
3 tsp. butter
½ tsp. ginger
2 tsp. sugar
Parsley to garnish

Cooking Instructions :

Boil carrots until tender. Dry thoroughly.
Heat butter and ginger in heavy skillet.
Roll carrots in sugar and place in skillet.
Simmer until glazed, turning frequently. Garnish with parsley.

Notes :

From the mess hall of Alola G. Morrison, Army Reserve and Public Health

Recipe : Herbed Rice

DIFFICULTY:

RATING:

PREP TIME:

COOK TIME:

Ingredients:

1 c. uncooked white rice
¼ c. butter
¼ c. onion, chopped
½ tsp. thyme, oregano, marjoram and parsley
2 chicken bullion cubes
2 x 2 2/3 c. boiling water

Cooking Instructions :

In a medium frying pan, melt butter and place rice.
Mix with butter and onions.
Cook over medium heat, stirring frequently. (do not let burn).
Add seasonings and bouillon after rice has browned.
Add boiling water and stir and then cover. Cook on low heat
until rice has absorbed the water.
Optional: Add shrimp or cooked pork chunks for a hardier dish.

Notes :

Serves 6.

From the mess hall of Alola Morrison's mother-in-law, Annette
Morrison.

Recipe : Irish Potatoes

Ingredients:

4 oz. cream cheese
4 tbsp. butter (1/2 stick)
1 tsp. vanilla
1 lb. powdered sugar
7 oz coconut

Cooking Instructions :

Cream together cream cheese, butter, vanilla. Then add powdered sugar and coconut. Mix well.

Roll into potato shapes.

Place 2 tsp. of cinnamon into a small bowl and roll the balls to cover, then chill.

Notes :

From the mess hall of Judy Colanino. Submitted by Shirley Merrill.

Recipe: Marinated Carrots (Copper Pennies)

DIFFICULTY:

RATING:

PREP TIME:

COOK TIME:

Ingredients:

2 lbs. carrots, peeled, cut
 and cooked in water and drained
1 sweet onion sliced
1 bell pepper, sliced
Mix above with drained carrots.

Sauce: 1 c. sugar
1/3 c. vegetable oil
½ cup vinegar
1 tsp. salt
1 tsp. pepper
1 tsp. dry mustard
1 can tomato soup

Cooking Instructions :

Bring sauce to a boil. Pour over carrot mix.
Can be served hot or cold.

Notes :

Brought to you from the mess hall of Gerry Kauth.

Recipe : Onion Casserole

DIFFICULTY:

RATING:

PREP TIME:

COOK TIME:

Ingredients:

3 or 4 med. yellow onions
1 can mushroom soup
½ tsp. black pepper
½ tsp. salt

Cooking Instructions :

Peel and cut onions into ¾ inch thick slices.
Grease a medium casserole dish and place the onions into dish.
Sprinkle salt and pepper over the onions.
Spoon the soup over the onions.
Cover and bake 350 degrees for an hour.

Notes :

From the mess hall of Viola Giffin, Alola Morrison's mother, who was also a Coast Guard officer's wife.

Recipe : Scalloped Corn Casserole

DIFFICULTY:

RATING:

PREP TIME:

COOK TIME:

Ingredients:

1 can cream style whole corn
1 egg, beaten
½ c. milk
1 to 2 c. crushed cracker crumbs

Cooking Instructions :

Place corn in a greased med. Casserole dish. Mix with milk, egg and half of the cracker crumbs.
Sprinkle rest of cracker crumbs over the top.
Bake 350 degrees until set, approximately 30 to 45 minutes.

Notes :

From the mess hall of Viola Giffin, Alola Morrison's mother, who was also a Coast Guard officer's wife.

Recipe : Scalloped Potatoes

Ingredients:

6 med. potatoes
4 Tbsp. butter
4 Tbsp. flour
2 tsp. salt
2 ½ c. milk
1 ½ c. cheese

Cooking Instructions :

Peel potatoes and slice thin. Make white sauce of butter, flour, salt and milk.
When thickened, remove from range and add cheese.
Place sliced potatoes in casserole, cover with hot cheese sauce.
Bake uncovered at 375 for 1 ½ hours.

Notes :

From the mess hall of Shirley Merrill.

Recipe : Squash Casserole

DIFFICULTY:

RATING:

PREP TIME:

COOK TIME:

Ingredients:

2 boxes frozen squash
1 can cream of chicken soup
8 oz container sour cream
Sm. amount grated carrot and green cabbage
Dash of onion and garlic.
1 bag Pepperidge Farm breadcrumbs
1 stick butter

Cooking Instructions :

Defrost squash until softened.
Mix in chicken soup and sour cream.
Add optional vegetables.
Melt a stick of butter and add 2/3 of the bread crumb mix.
Combine the rest of the crumbs on the top of the casserole.

Notes :

Donated by one of our Veteran friends.

Recipe : Steamed Cabbage

DIFFICULTY:

RATING:

PREP TIME:

COOK TIME:

Ingredients:

¼ c. water
¼ c. butter
1 head of cabbage shredded
Pinch of salt
Dash of black pepper

Cooking Instructions :

Melt butter in large frying pan.
Put water in pan.
Place shredded cabbage in pan and cover.
Cook on high heat until it begins to steam. Stir and place on low heat for 15 to 20 minutes.
Add salt and pepper. Mix and serve hot.

Notes :

From the mess hall of Alola G. Morrison, Army Reserve and Public Health

DIFFICULTY:

RATING:

PREP TIME:

COOK TIME:

Ingredients:

2 cans sweet potatoes)1 lb. +) not glazed
1 can drained crushed pineapple
1/8 tsp. nutmeg
½ tsp. salt
2 tbsp. brown sugar
¼ c. butter, melted

Topping:
1/3 c. brown sugar
2 c. crushed corn flakes
½ c. melted butter.

Cooking Instructions :

Mash sweet potatoes until smooth. Mix with pineapple.
Place in a 1 ½ qt. greased baking dish.
Sprinkle topping over the mixture.
Bake uncovered 40 minutes at 325 degrees.

Topping:
Mix together ingredients and put on top of sweet potatoes and pineapples before baking.

Notes :

Serves 8 to 10.

From the mess hall of Alola G. Morrison, Army Reserve and Public Health

DIFFICULTY:

RATING:

PREP TIME:

COOK TIME:

Ingredients:

3 c. mashed sweet potatoes (about 4 med. potatoes)
½ c. brown sugar
½ stick butter
½ c. milk
½ tsp salt
1 to 2 eggs

Topping:
½ c. brown sugar
1 c. chopped pecans

Cooking Instructions :

Mix all together, add topping, and bake at 350 for 35 minutes.

Notes :

From the mess hall of Nina Braley.

Main Dishes

Recipe : Baked Fish Newburg

DIFFICULTY:

RATING:

PREP TIME:

COOK TIME:

Ingredients:

1 or 2 lbs. fish sticks (boiled 10 minutes)
White Sauce:
2 Tbsp. butter
2 Tbsp. flour
1 c. milk

Then add:
1/8 cheese
2 Tbsp. sherry
¾ tsp. salt
Buttered breadcrumbs

Cooking Instructions :

Bake at 375° for 20-30 minutes.

Notes :

From one of our Veteran friends.

Recipe : BBQ Jackfruit "Pulled Pork"

DIFFICULTY:

RATING:

PREP TIME:

COOK TIME:

Ingredients:

40 oz. canned jackfruit in water
1 lg. onion, diced
1 Tbsp. olive oil
1 tbsp. minced garlic
2 tbsp. Chili powder
2 tbsp. brown sugar

1 tbsp. paprika (salted)
1 tsp. cumin
Salt and black pepper to taste
1 c. BBQ Sauce
Water as needed

Cooking Instructions :

Drain jackfruit. Rinse sell. Break apart by hand.
Heat oil, sauté onion and jackfruit until lightly caramelized.
Add remaining ingredients, except BBQ sauce.
Sauté 10 minutes on medium heat.
Add sauce.

Notes :

From the kitchen of Patricia Learned.

Recipe : Chinese Style Casserole

DIFFICULTY:

RATING:

PREP TIME:

COOK TIME:

Ingredients:

1 can tuna or chicken
1 can cream of mushroom soup
¼ c. water
1 can Chinese crisp noodles
¼ lb. cashew nuts

Cooking Instructions :

Mix all ingredients saving a few noodles to sprinkle on top.
Bake at 350° for 1 hour.

Notes :

From the mess hall from one of our Veteran friends.

Recipe : Chicken & Broccoli Alfredo

DIFFICULTY:

RATING:

PREP TIME:

COOK TIME:

Ingredients:

½ of a 1 lb. pkg. Linguine
1 c. fresh or frozen broccoli
florets
2 Tbsp. butter
1 ¼ lb. skinless, boneless chicken
Breast halves, cut into 1 ½" pieces

1 can (10 ¾ oz) cream of
mushroom soup
½ c. milk
½ c. grated parmesan cheese
¼ tsp. ground black pepper

Cooking Instructions :

Prepare linguine according to package directions in 3-qt saucepan.
Add broccoli during last 4 min. of cooking time. Drain linguine
mixture well in colander.
Heat butter in 10" skillet over medium-high heat. Add chicken and
cook until well browned and cooked through, stirring often.
Stir soup, milk, cheese, black pepper and linguine mixture in skillet
and cook until mixture is hot and bubbling, stirring occasionally.
Serve with additional parmesan cheese.

Notes :

From the mess hall of Jerry Black.

Recipe : Cream Tuna on Rice

DIFFICULTY:

RATING:

PREP TIME: 5-minute meal

COOK TIME:

Ingredients:

6 Tbsp. flour
Dash salt and pepper
6 Tbsp. butter
2 c. milk
1 can drained tuna

Cooking Instructions :

Melt butter slowly and add flour mixture and stir until creamy.
Remove from heat. Add milk slowly. Put back on medium heat,
Stirring constantly until it begins to boil and thickens.
Drain tuna and add in. Pour white sauce over rice.
Pairs well with peas.

Notes :

From the mess hall of Rita.

Recipe : Easy Cheesy Chicken Bake

DIFFICULTY:

RATING:

PREP TIME:

COOK TIME: 35 minutes

Ingredients:

1 - 1½ chicken breast cut into bite size pieces
1 - 14oz frozen broccoli thawed and drained
1 can cream of chicken soup
½ c. milk

1 c. shredded cheddar cheese
Sprinkle of onion powder
1 box Stovetop Stuffing

Cooking Instructions :

Mix above ingredients together (except the stuffing).
Put in a 9x13 pan.
Fix stuffing per box instructions and spread on the top of chicken mixture.
Bake at 400° in 30-35 minutes – until chicken is cooked and mixture is bubbly.

Notes :

From the mess hall of Clarence Cummings.

Recipe : Easy Parmesan Garlic Chicken

DIFFICULTY:

RATING:

PREP TIME:

COOK TIME:

Ingredients:

½ c. grated parmesan cheese
1 envelope Good Seasons Dressing Dry
6 boneless chicken breasts halves (approx. 2 lbs.)
½ tsp. garlic powder

Cooking Instructions :

Mix cheese, garlic, butter and salad mix.
Moisten chicken with water then add cheese mixture.

Notes :

Serves 6.

From the mess hall of Nina Braley.

Recipe : Fish Chowder

DIFFICULTY:

RATING:

PREP TIME:

COOK TIME:

Ingredients:

2 lbs. fish fillets (haddock, cod)
½ c. margarine
2 onions, finely cut
4 c. potatoes cut into ½ inch cubes
1 to 2 c. water
2 c. whole milk

1 - 15 oz. can evaporated milk, heated
1 tsp. salt
½ tsp. pepper

Cooking Instructions :

In a large skillet, sauté onions in the margarine until opaque.
Add the potatoes and enough water to be seen around potatoes,
Not quite covering them. Cook until potatoes are semisoft. Place
Fish on top of the potatoes and sprinkle the salt and pepper over
The fish. Cover and bring to a boil. Lower heat and cook 7 to 10
minutes. Fish should easily flake. Add both kinds of milk. Taste for
seasoning., adding more salt and pepper, if desired. Heat
thoroughly, but do not boil. Stir gently to keep fish in large chunks.

Notes :

Serves 6 to 8.
Hint: Chowder tastes better if made one day ahead,
refrigerated and slowly reheated to serve.

Pam Whynot approves of this recipe.

Recipe : Ground Beef Casserole

DIFFICULTY:

RATING:

PREP TIME:

COOK TIME:

Ingredients:

1 lb. ground beef
1/3 c. chopped onion
1 Tbsp. chile powder
1 can tomato sauce
1 c. diced green pepper
10 oz. pkg. frozen corn
½ c. water

Cooking Instructions :

Brown ¾ c. of beef and chopped onion.
Drain and add sauce, water, corn, green pepper, chile powder until mixed and hot.
Make a cup of Minute Rice and then blend rice into the beef mixture.
Add parmesan cheese, if you want.

Notes :

Donated by one of our Veteran friends.

Recipe : Italian Meatloaf

DIFFICULTY:

RATING:

PREP TIME:

COOK TIME: 1 hour 15 min.

Ingredients:

1 ½ lbs. ground meat
1 egg beaten
¾ c. cracker crumbs
½ c. chopped onions
1 tsp. salt
1/3 c. tomato sauce

½ tsp. oregano
¼ tsp. pepper
2. c. grated mozzarella cheese
2/3 c. tomato sauce

Cooking Instructions :

Combine meat, egg, cracker crumbs, onion the 1/3 c. tomato
sauce, salt, oregano, pepper. Shape into a 10x12 rectangle pan
lined with wax paper.
Sprinkle with the cheese. Roll up and press ends to seal.
Place in a shallow pan and bake 1 hour at 350 degrees.
Pour the 2/3 c. of sauce over the top and bake another 15 minutes.

Notes :

From the mess hall of Miriam B. Lao. Shared by Shirley Merrill.

Recipe : Pork Chop Chasseur

DIFFICULTY:

RATING:

PREP TIME:

COOK TIME:

Ingredients:

16 oz. tomatoes
6 pork chops (about 2 pounds)
1 can golden cream of mushroom soup
1/3 chopped onion
2 tsp. mustard
1/8 – ¼ tsp. pepper

½ c. dill or sweet sliced pickles
3 c. cooked hot rice

Cooking Instructions :

Drain tomatoes. Reserve ½ c. liquid. Cut up tomatoes. In skillet brown chops. Take off excess fat. Add to soup, reserve tomatoes juice, onion, mustard and pepper.
Cook over low heat for 30 minutes or until done.
Stir occasionally. Add tomatoes and pickles last.
Heat.
Serve over rice with parsley.

Notes :

From the mess hall of Celeste Kennedy and Moe.

Recipe : Red Flannel Hash

DIFFICULTY:

RATING:

PREP TIME:

COOK TIME:

Ingredients:

2. tbsp. butter
1 chopped onion, medium
2 med. potatoes, chopped
Approx. 1 c. beets, chopped
Approx.. 1 c. rutabagas, chopped
1 c. cooked cabbage, chopped

1 c. cooked carrots, chopped
1 tsp. salt
½ tsp. pepper

Cooking Instructions :

This hash is a choose and mix or use everything. It's a leftover meal so what you have on hand for left over vegetables just might taste good. The listed ingredients are standard fare.
Sauté the onion in butter.
Add all of the vegetables which should be chopped finely or mashed. Fry all of the ingredients together in a fry pan. Adjust salt and pepper to personal taste.

Notes :

From the mess hall of Pam Whynot.

Recipe : Sh*t on a Shingle

DIFFICULTY:

RATING:

PREP TIME:

COOK TIME:

Ingredients:

1 med. Yellow onion, ¼ inch pieces
¼ tsp. salt
1 to 2 Tbsp. cooking oil
2 Tbsp. flour
2 med. button mushrooms chopped
Toast, crackers, English Muffin

1 to 1 ½ c. milk (not skim)
1 c. grated sharp cheese
1 lb. hamburger

Cooking Instructions :

Brown hamburg, onions, and mushrooms with 1 to 2 Tbsp. of oil
on medium heat.
When brown add salt and pepper and flour on top and mix.
Meat should be covered with flour. Turn to low and add milk.
Stir until thickened. Can add more milk if too thick.
Pour over toasted bread or what you want to use.
Add cheese at the last moment before pouring over bread.

Notes :

Total servings 6.

From the mess hall of Alola Morrison.

Recipe : Spaghetti Pie

DIFFICULTY:

RATING:

PREP TIME:

COOK TIME:

Ingredients:

6 oz. cooked spaghetti
2 tbsp. butter
2 beaten eggs
1/3 c. parmesan cheese
1 c. cream-style cottage cheese
1 lb. bulk pork or Italian sausage
or hamburger or a combo

1 c. Italian sauce
1 – 6 oz. can tomato paste
2 oz. shredded mozzarella cheese
¼ c. each onion and green pepper

Cooking Instructions :

Stir butter into hot spaghetti. Stir in beaten eggs and parmesan cheese. Form spaghetti mixture into a crust in a greased 10 in. pie plate. Spread with cottage cheese.

In skillet, cook sausage, onion and green pepper until meat is browned and veggies are tender. Drain off fat. Stir in Italian sauce and tomato paste. Heat through. Turn meat mixture into spaghetti crust. Cover edges with foil. Bake at 350 for 20 minutes. Sprinkle with mozzarella. Bake about 5 min. until melted.

Notes :

For crunchy texture for the crust, remove foil during last 5 minutes.

From the mess hall of Shirley Merrill.

Recipe : Spaghetti Sauce and Meatballs

DIFFICULTY:

RATING:

PREP TIME:

COOK TIME:

Ingredients:

3 - 29 oz. cans tomato sauce
4-5 minced garlic cloves
1 med. onion
1 stalk celery with leaves
1 tsp. sugar
2-3 bay leaves
1 tsp. basil
1 Tbsp. Italian seasoning.

Meatballs: 2 -3 lbs. ground chuck
1 med. onion chopped
1 tsp. garlic powder
3 eggs
3 Tbsp. parmesan cheese
1 c. crackers or breadcrumbs

Cooking Instructions :

For the sauce: Add all the ingredients, mix and simmer for 4 to 6 hours. Stir occasionally.
While sauce is simmering, make the meatballs.

To make the meatballs:
Mix together, then add the cup of breadcrumbs or crackers crushed.
Bake for 15 minutes at 400 degrees.
Then add to sauce.

Notes :

From the mess hall of Pam Plescher by way of Celeste Kennedy.

Recipe : Tahini Noodles

DIFFICULTY:

RATING:

PREP TIME:

COOK TIME:

Ingredients:

½ c. Braggs Amino
½ c. Tahini
½ Tbsp. grated fresh ginger or frozen peeled ginger
2 cloves minced fresh garlic
3 Tbsp. Agave syrup

¼ c. rice wine vinegar
2 tsp. Sriracha sauce
1 tsp. ground black pepper
1 lb. spaghetti

Cooking Instructions :

Cook pasta.
Place ingredients in blender until creamy.
Pour over pasta.
May top with grated carrots or thinly sliced scallions.

Notes :

From the mess hall of Jeanne Fiske.

Recipe : Vegan stuffed peppers

Ingredients:

1 package Beyond Burgers
1 lg. onion, red or yellow
¼ pkg. cherry tomatoes, halved
1 pkg. Knorr Rice Sides
chicken flavor
1 tbsp. butter

1 tbsp. parsley
½ tsp. garlic salt
Salt and pepper to taste
½ jar marinara sauce

Cooking Instructions :

Preheat oven 400.
Spray pan with Pam, add ½ cup water.
In skillet, brown vegan burger meat mixture, chopped onion and then halved tomatoes.
As that is cooling, prepare Knorr Rice according to package directions.
Add cooked rice to vegan meat mixture and almost half jar marinara sauce, saving some to top off the stuffed peppers.
Stuff the peppers and top with marinara sauce. Cook 50-60 minutes at 400.

Notes :

Can be frozen or refrigerated.

From the kitchen of Patricia Learned.

Recipe : Valentino's Pizza Crust

DIFFICULTY:

RATING: 5/5

PREP TIME:

COOK TIME:

Ingredients:

- 1 c. warm water
- 1 Tbsp. sugar
- 2 ¼ tsp. active dry yeast
- 3 Tbsp. olive oil
- 1 tsp. salt
- 2 ½ c. flour

Cooking Instructions :

Stir warm water, sugar and yeast together until dissolved. Let the
yeast work and get bubbly. Add olive oil and salt. Stir in flour
until well blended. Let dough sit for 10 minutes.
Pat dough on a pizza pan or stone. If sticky you can dip your fingers
in olive oil. Top your pizza with desired toppings and lots of cheese.

Bake for 18 minutes or until golden in a 450 oven.

Notes :

You can add basil, thyme or pizza seasonings on the crust for a
different flavor.

From the mess hall of Lisa DeFosse. Submitted by Michelle Libby

Desserts

Recipe : Apple Crisp

DIFFICULTY:

RATING:

PREP TIME:

COOK TIME:

Ingredients:

¾ c. Quick rolled oats
¾ c brown sugar
½ c. flour
½ tsp. cinnamon
½ c. butter
4 cups apple

Cooking Instructions :

Combine oats, sugar, flour, cinnamon and cut in butter.
Put apples in 8" pan. Sprinkle over.

Bake at 375° for 35 minutes. Serves 6.

Notes :

From the mess hall of Betsy Black.

Recipe : Apple Dumpling Pie

DIFFICULTY:

RATING:

PREP TIME:

COOK TIME:

Ingredients:

8 to 10 apples sliced
1 tsp. sugar
1 tsp. cinnamon

1 stick butter, melted
1 egg
1 c. flour
1 c. sugar
Dash salt
Squirt lemon

Cooking Instructions :

Grease pie plate. Put first three ingredients in pie pan.
Beat rest of ingredients together. Pour over apples.
Cook for 35 to 40 minutes at 350 degrees.

Notes :

From the mess hall of Shirley Merrill.

Ingredients:

½ c. sugar
½ tsp soda
Salt
1 c. flour
1 tsp. cream of tartar
nutmeg

Cooking Instructions :

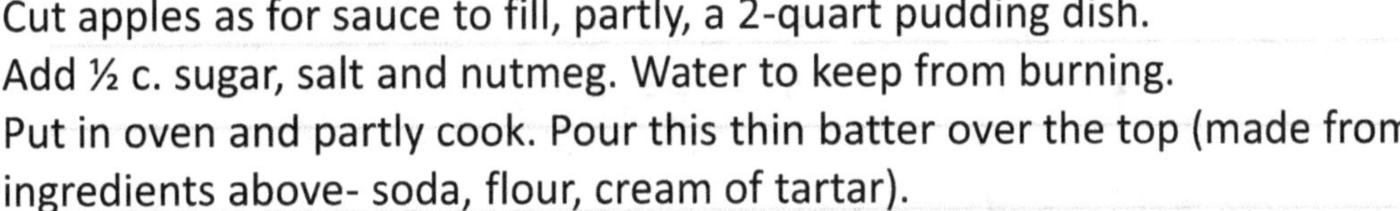

Cut apples as for sauce to fill, partly, a 2-quart pudding dish.
Add ½ c. sugar, salt and nutmeg. Water to keep from burning.
Put in oven and partly cook. Pour this thin batter over the top (made from ingredients above- soda, flour, cream of tartar).

Notes :

From the mess hall of one of our Veteran friend.

Recipe : Applesauce Cake

DIFFICULTY:

RATING:

PREP TIME:

COOK TIME:

Ingredients:

2 ½ c. sifted flour	½ tsp. ground cloves
1 ½ c. sugar	½ c. butter
¼ tsp. baking powder	½ c. water
1 ½ tsp. baking soda	2 c. sweetened applesauce
1 ½ tsp. salt	2 eggs
¾ tsp. cinnamon	1 c. raisins
½ tsp. allspice	¾ c. chopped nuts

Cooking Instructions :

Sift dry ingredients together 3 times. Add butter, water, and applesauce. Beat 2 minutes at medium speed.
Add eggs: beat 2 more minutes. Add raisins, making sure they are well blended. Fold in nuts.
Bake in greased 13x9 pan for 45 to 50 minutes at 350.
When cool sprinkle with confectioners' sugar or frosting of your choice.

Notes :

From the mess hall of Sue Roeder. Submitted by Shirley Merrill.

Recipe : Apple Walnut Supreme Cake

Ingredients:

4 c. coarsely chopped peeled apples
1 ¾ c. sugar
2 c. sifted all-purpose flour
2 tsp. baking soda
1 tsp. salt

2 tsp. cinnamon
2 eggs
½ c. vegetable oil
2 tsp. vanilla
½ c. chopped walnuts

Cooking Instructions :

Preheat oven to 350°
Combine apples and sugar, set aside.
Whisk together flour, baking soda, salt, and cinnamon, set aside. In a large mixing bowl mix eggs, oil, and vanilla; then beat one minute at medium speed. Add combined dry ingredients alternately with apple mixture. Stir in walnuts. Pour into a greased and floured 13x9x2 pan. Bake for 45-50 minutes. Test with a toothpick. If desired, drizzle top of cooled cake with lemon glaze.

Notes :

From the mess hall of Elizabeth Bailey.

Lemon glaze: 1 c. confectioner's sugar, 1 ½ Tbsp. lemon juice, ½ tsp. Vanilla and 1 Tbsp. corn syrup until smooth.

Recipe : Blueberry Sour Cream Cake

DIFFICULTY:

RATING:

PREP TIME:

COOK TIME:

Ingredients:

½ c. butter
1 c. sugar
3 eggs
1 c. sour cream
1 tsp. Vanilla
2 c. flour
½ tsp. salt

1 tsp. baking soda
2 c. blueberries rinsed, strained and floured
½ c. brown sugar
½ c. nuts, optional
½ tsp. cinnamon

Cooking Instructions :

Cream butter until light and fluffy. Beat in sugar, beat in eggs. Stir
In sour cream and vanilla. Add flour, baking soda and salt until well
combined. Fold in blueberries. Pour ½ batter into 9x13 pan.
In a separate bowl, mix brown sugar and cinnamon. Sprinkle on
top of batter in 9x13. Top with the rest of the batter.
For the topping, repeat brown sugar and cinnamon. Add 1 to 2 Tbsp.
Spoon on top. Bake at 350 for 40 minutes or until done
with toothpick.

Notes :

From the mess hall from Donna Lynne Nickerson, via Shirley Merrill.

Recipe : Chocolate Fudge

DIFFICULTY:

RATING:

PREP TIME:

COOK TIME:

Ingredients:

4 c. sugar
1 lg. can evaporated milk
1 c. butter.

12 oz. pkg. semisweet chocolate
2 c. marshmallow fluff
1 tsp. vanilla
1 c. broken walnuts (optional)

Cooking Instructions :

Butter sides of a 3 qt. saucepan. Add in sugar, evaporated milk
and butter. Cook over medium high heat to softball stage
(236 degrees).
Stirring frequently. Remove from heat.
Mix in chocolate, marshmallow and vanilla. (And, walnuts.)
Beat until chocolate melts. Pour into buttered 13x9x2 pan.
Score while warm. Cut when cool and firm.

Notes :

From the mess hall from Shirley Merrill.

Recipe : Chocolate Oatmeal Cake

DIFFICULTY:

RATING:

PREP TIME:

COOK TIME: 35 minutes

Ingredients:

1 c. Quick Cooking Oats
1 ½ c. boiling water
½ c. shortening
1 ½ c. sugar
2 eggs
1 c. flour

½ c. cocoa
1 tsp. soda
½ tsp. salt
1 tsp. vanilla

Cooking Instructions :

Mix oats in water and cool. Cream shortening, sugar and eggs.
Add to oatmeal mixture. Along with the dry ingredients.
Add vanilla. Beat until smooth. Bake in greased 9x12 pan.
Cook at 35 minutes @ 350 degrees.

It will pull away from the sides when done.

Notes :

From the mess hall of Donna Cote.

Recipe : Cottage Pudding	DIFFICULTY: RATING: PREP TIME: COOK TIME:

Ingredients:

¼ c. shortening
¾ c. sugar
½ tsp. vanilla
2 eggs
1 2/3 c. sifted flour

2 tsp. baking powder
½ tsp. salt
¾ c. milk

Cooking Instructions :

Mix together.
Bake at 375°

Notes :

From the mess hall of Betsy Black.

Recipe : Crunchy Fudge Sandwich

DIFFICULTY:

RATING:

PREP TIME:

COOK TIME:

Ingredients:

6 oz. pkg. butterscotch bits
½ c. peanut butter
4 c. Rice Krispies

Topping:
6 oz. chocolate bits
½ c. confectioners' sugar
2 tbsp. butter
1 tbsp. water

Cooking Instructions :

Melt together butterscotch bits and peanut butter.
Stir in the Rice Krispies.
Press half of mixture into 8x8 pan and chill in refrigerator.

Topping: Stir chocolate and other topping ingredients over hot
water. Cook until melted and spread over Rice Krispies mixture.
Add rest of mixture on top.
Use an 8x8 buttered pan.

Notes :

From the mess hall of Nina Braley.

Recipe : Delightful Chocolate Cake

DIFFICULTY:

RATING:

PREP TIME:

COOK TIME:

Ingredients:

1 German chocolate cake mix (Prepare according to directions.)
1 c. chopped pecans
1 c. shredded coconut
8 oz. cream cheese, softened
1 stick butter
1lb. Confectioners sugar

Cooking Instructions :

Preheat oven to 350.
Spray bottom of 9x13 baking dish. Sprinkle pecans and coconut
over bottom. Prepare cake mix and pour gently over pecans and
coconut.
Mix cream cheese, butter and confectioners' sugar with mixer.
Pour over top of cake leaving an edge of about ½ inch.
Bake at 350 for 50 minutes.

Notes :

Serve warm with ice cream or Cool Whip.

From the mess hall of Anne Stratton. Submitted by Shirley Merrill.

DIFFICULTY:

RATING:

PREP TIME:

COOK TIME: 15 minutes

Ingredients:

2 c. raisins
1 c. water
1 c. applesauce
2 eggs
¾ c. cooking oil
Sugar substitute to equal
1 c. sugar

1 tsp. vanilla
2 c. flour
1 tsp. baking soda
½ tsp salt
1 ½ tsp. cinnamon
½ c. walnuts

Cooking Instructions :

Cook raisins in water until soft. Drain off water! Set aside to cool. Mix applesauce, eggs, sweetener, vanilla, and cooking oil very well. Add dry ingredients and stir well. Add raisins and nuts. Spoon into cupcake papered pans. Bake at 350° until toothpick comes out clean, about 15 minutes. Makes about 2 dozen.

One cupcake equals 1 fruit and 1 fat.

Notes :

From the mess hall of Mildred Black

Recipe : Devil Dog Recipe

Ingredients:

1 c. butter
2 c. sugar
2 eggs
4 c. flour
1 c. cocoa
3 tsp. baking soda

1 tsp. salt
2 tsp. vanilla
2 c. milk

Filling: 5 tbsp. flour, 1 c. milk,
1 c. Crisco, 1 c. sugar, ½ tsp. salt
1 tsp. vanilla.

Cooking Instructions :

Cream butter and sugar. Mix in remaining ingredients. Drop by
heaping teaspoons onto cookie sheet.

Bake 7 to 8 minutes at 425. Let cool.

Filling: Cook flour and milk until thick...stirring constantly. Cool.
Cream together the shortening, sugar, salt and vanilla. Add flour
Mixture. Beat well until very smooth and not grainy. Drop onto
Cooled Devil Dogs. Top with another Devil Dog.

Notes :

You don't have to add the eggs and it will be more like a brownie.
These freeze well. You can also try different filling recipes.

From the mess hall library of Michelle Libby.

Recipe : Dump Cake

DIFFICULTY:

RATING:

PREP TIME:

COOK TIME:

Ingredients:

1 lg. can crushed pineapple with juice
1 can cherry pie filling
1 yellow cake mix
½ c. butter
½ c. nuts chopped

Cooking Instructions :

Dump pineapple into well creased cake pan
Dump cherry pie filling over pineapple. Spread yellow cake mix
(dry) over pineapple and cherry mixture. Slice butter and put on
top of cake mix.
Bake for 45 minutes at 350 in a 13x9 pan until top is a little
brown and sort of hard.

Notes :

Serve with whipped cream or Cool Whip.

From the mess hall of Shirley Merrill.

Recipe : Éclair Cake

DIFFICULTY:

RATING:

PREP TIME:

COOK TIME:

Ingredients:

1 box graham crackers
2 sm. Pkg instant vanilla pudding
1 – 8 oz. Cool Whip
3 ½ c. milk
1 can chocolate frosting

Cooking Instructions :

Mix the milk with the vanilla pudding then fold in the Cool Whip.
Layer the pudding mixture and the graham crackers until you run out.
Top with chocolate frosting. It works best to frost the graham crackers,
then add them to the top of the cake.

Refrigerate for 6 hours or overnight.

Cut and serve.

Notes :

This is a crowd favorite.

From the mess hall of Michelle Libby.

Recipe : Eggnog Sauce

DIFFICULTY:

RATING:

PREP TIME:

COOK TIME:

Ingredients:

2 tsp. cornstarch
1/8 tsp. salt
1 ½ cups dairy eggnog

2 tsp. bandy extract
½ tsp. rum extract

Cooking Instructions :

Combine cornstarch and salt in a 1-quart saucepan; gradually stir in eggnog. Cook over medium hear, stirring constantly, until thickened. Boil and stir, occasionally, 2 additional minutes. Remove from heat; stir in extracts. Chill. Serve with Steamed Date Pudding.

Notes :

From the mess hall of one of our Veteran friends.

Recipe : Flourless Cookies

DIFFICULTY:

RATING:

PREP TIME:

COOK TIME:

Ingredients:

1 c. brown sugar
1 ¼ tsp. baking soda
1 tsp. vanilla
1 c. peanut butter
2 eggs
¾ c. chocolate chips

Cooking Instructions :

Blend brown sugar and peanut butter in mixer. Add eggs, spoon
in baking soda and vanilla.
Drop by tsp. on grease cookie sheet.
Cook at 350 for 10 minutes.

Notes :

From the mess hall of Nina Braley.

Recipe : Fresh Strawberry Pie

DIFFICULTY:

RATING:

PREP TIME:

COOK TIME:

Ingredients:

3 c. fresh sliced strawberries
1 to 1 ½ c. sugar
¼ c. flour
Dash of salt
2 Tbsp. butter

Cooking Instructions :

Turn into a pastry lined pie plate. Dot with 2 tbsp. butter.
Add top crust. Slit to release steam. Bake at 400 for
50 to 55 minutes.

Notes :

From the mess hall of Shirley Merrill.

Recipe : Great Grandmother Jordan's Molasses Cookies

Ingredients:

1 c. granulated sugar
1 c. molasses
1 c. water
1 rounded tsp. salt
Approx. 6 c. sifted flour

¾ c shortening (melted)
2 rounded tsp. baking soda
1 level tsp. cream of tartar
1 tsp. each of ginger, nutmeg, cinnamon

Cooking Instructions :

Chill over night, mixture should be soft enough to roll out. Roll ¼ ".
Bake 375° 10 to 12 minutes until done.
Yield: 6 dozen large

Original recipe called for 1 ¼ c. beef drippings.

Notes :

From the mess hall of Craig Pride.

Recipe : Ginger Snap Yummies

DIFFICULTY:

RATING:

PREP TIME:

COOK TIME:

Ingredients:

¾ c. Crisco
1 1/3 c. sugar (separated)
1 egg
¼ c. light molasses
2 tsp. baking soda
2 c. flour
¼ tsp. salt

1 tsp. cinnamon
1 tsp. ground cloves
1 tsp. ground ginger

Cooking Instructions :

Cream Crisco with 1 c. sugar. Add egg and molasses. Beat well.
Mix in rest of ingredients except 1/3 c. sugar. Shape into small
balls. Roll balls in 1/3 c. sugar. Place on cookie sheet.
Bake 10 to 12 minutes in 375 degree oven. Makes 24 to 27
cookies depending on size of ball.

Notes :

From the mess hall of Gail Labbe.

Recipe : Gluten free Lemon Squares with Almond Flour Crust

Ingredients:

Crust:
2 c. almond flour
3 Tbsp. cornstarch
6 Tbsp. sugar
6 Tbsp. cold butter
Dash salt

Filling:
2 lg. eggs
1 c. sugar
1/3 c. lemon juice
2 Tbsp. cornstarch

Cooking Instructions :

Crust: Combine dry ingredients, blend in cold butter with fingers.
Press crust down and upwards of pan.
Bake 8 to 10 minutes
Remove from oven. Pour filing on crust.
Bake 14 to 18 minutes at 350 for 14 to 18 additional minutes.
Refrigerate until ready to serve.

Notes :

Makes 16 squares.

From the mess hall of Nina Braley.

Recipe : Hermits

DIFFICULTY:

RATING:

PREP TIME:

COOK TIME: 15 minutes

Ingredients:

1 c shortening
2 c. brown sugar
2 well-beaten eggs
3 ½ c. flour
½ tsp. salt
1 tsp. baking powder

1 tsp. soda
2 tsp. cinnamon
1 tsp. nutmeg
½ c. sour milk
1 c. seeded raisins
1 c. chopped dates
1 c. broken nut meats

Cooking Instructions :

Cream shortening and sugar; add eggs and beat well.
Add sifted dry ingredients alternately with sour milk.
Add fruits and nut meats.
Drop from teaspoon onto greased cookie sheet.
Bake in moderate oven (375°) 15 minutes.

Makes 4 dozen cookies.

Notes :

From the mess hall of one of our Veteran friends.

Recipe : Lemon Cookies

DIFFICULTY:

RATING:

PREP TIME:

COOK TIME: 12 to 15 min.

Ingredients:

1 pkg. (1 ½ oz) whipped topping mix
1 pkg. (1lb. 3 oz.) lemon cake mix
1 egg
1 c. confectioners' sugar

Cooking Instructions :

Preheat oven to 350 degrees.
Prepare whipped topping mix according to package directions.
Add cake mix, egg and mix until well blended and smooth.
Drop by teaspoonful onto confectioners' sugar.
Shape into small balls.
Place on a lightly greased cookie sheet.
Bake for 12 to 15 minutes or until done.
Remove and cool on wire racks.

Notes :

Makes 3 dozen.

From the Mess hall of Shirley Merrill.

Recipe : Lemon Squares

DIFFICULTY:

RATING:

PREP TIME:

COOK TIME:

Ingredients:

2 c. four
½ c. confectioners sugar
2 sticks of butter

4 beaten eggs
2 c. sugar
1/3 c. lemon juice (1 to 2 lemons)
¼ c. flour (rounded)
½ tsp. baking powder
Dash salt

Cooking Instructions :

Take first three ingredients, mix, and bake at 350 for
20 to 25 minutes in 9 x 13 pan

Beat eggs. Gradually add sugar, lemon juice, sifted ingredients and
Pour over crust. Bake at 350 for 25 minutes or longer. Sprinkle with
Confectioner sugar over top.

Notes :

From the mess hall of Shirley Merrill.

Recipe : Maine Blueberry Pie

DIFFICULTY:

RATING:

PREP TIME:

COOK TIME: 40 minutes

Ingredients:

4 c. blueberries
¼ tsp. nutmeg
1 c. sugar
¼ tsp. cinnamon

2 Tbsp. flour
1 Tbsp. butter
Dash of salt

Cooking Instructions :

Preheat oven to 425°. Line pie plate with pastry.
Mix sugar and flour, spread about ¼ of it on lower crust.
Fill with blueberries.
Sprinkle remainder of sugar mix over them.
Add salt; sprinklewith nutmeg and cinnamon. Dot butter.
Place top crust on pie, flute edges, and cut slits.
Bake for 40 minutes.

Notes :

From the mess hall of Mildred Black.

Recipe : Molasses Cookies

DIFFICULTY:

RATING:

PREP TIME:

COOK TIME: 15 minutes

Ingredients:

¾ c. shortening
1 c. sugar
2 well-beaten eggs
1 c. light molasses
4 c. flour

1 tsp. salt
1 tsp. soda
2 tsp. cinnamon
1 tsp. ginger
¾ c. cold strong coffee

Cooking Instructions :

Thoroughly cream shortening and sugar; add eggs and molasses.
Beat well. Add sifted dry ingredients alternately with coffee.
Drop from teaspoon onto greased cookie sheet.
Bake in moderate oven (350°) 15 minutes.

Makes 7 dozen cookies.

Notes :

From the mess hall of one of our Veteran friend.

Recipe : Molasses Cookies / Sophie's Cookies

DIFFICULTY:

RATING:

PREP TIME:

COOK TIME: 10-12 minutes

Ingredients:

1 c. melted Crisco
1 c. brown sugar
1 c. molasses
1 egg
salt
1 tsp. baking soda

4 c. flour
½ tsp. cinnamon
¼ tsp. cloves (ground)
¼ tsp. nutmeg

Cooking Instructions :

Add 1 cup boiling water, salt, and soda to first four ingredients.
Mix in remaining dry ingredients.

Bake in a 350 degree oven for 10-12 minutes.

Notes :

From the mess hall of Pat Salmon.

Recipe : New Hermits

DIFFICULTY:

RATING:

PREP TIME:

COOK TIME: 40 minutes

Ingredients:

1 c. evaporated milk
1 Tbsp. vinegar
½ c. shortening
2 c. brown sugar, well-packed
½ tsp. salt
2 eggs
½ tsp. vanilla

2 Tbsp c. sifted flour
1 tsp. soda
1 tsp. cinnamon
1 tsp. powdered cloves
1 tsp. allspice
¼ tsp. nutmeg
3 c. or 1 lb. seedless raisins
½ c. chopped nuts

Cooking Instructions :

Mix milk and vinegar together and let stand. Cream shortening,
add sugar gradually, add salt and vanilla. Add eggs one at a time,
beating well after each addition. Sift dry ingredients together and
add to creamed mixture with evaporated milk mixture.
Stir in raisins and chopped nuts. Drop by teaspoonfuls onto
greased cookie sheets. Bake at 350 degrees about 15 minutes.
Makes about 6 dozen cookies.

Notes :

From the mess hall of Jerry Black.

Recipe : Peanut Butter Fudge

Nina Braley's Famous

DIFFICULTY:

RATING:

PREP TIME:

COOK TIME:

Ingredients:

1 stick butter
1 lb. light brown sugar (2 cups)
1 lb. confectionary sugar (3 ½ cups)
1 c. evaporated milk (not one can)
1 jar (8 ½ oz.) marshmallow
2 c. peanut butter
1 tsp. vanilla

Cooking Instructions :

Melt butter in saucepan and add milk. Stir in brown sugar and confectionary sugar until smooth...bring to a boil...boil for 4 minutes stirring constantly. When it starts to boil, remove from the heat and add vanilla, peanut butter, and fluff. (Don't take too long at this point or the fudge will harden in the pan.) Stir (stir is probably not what you need here – beat vigorously is more like it, in fact at this point you would have benefitted greatly from a few months of weight training at the local gym) until smooth and pour into buttered pan (spray with Pam) Pan 9x13.
Cool in fridge for 2 hours, then cut.

Notes :

From the mess hall of Nina Braley. She used to make this fudge for BINGO nights and it would sell out immediately.

Recipe : Orange Drop Cookies

DIFFICULTY:

RATING:

PREP TIME:

COOK TIME: 15 minutes

Ingredients:

¾ c shortening
¼ c. butter
1 ½ c. brown sugar
2 well-beaten eggs
¼ c. orange juice
1 Tbsp. grated orange peel
1 tsp. vanilla extract

1 c. sour milk
3 ½ c. flour
¼ tsp. salt
2 tsp. baking powder
1 tsp. soda
1 c. chopped dates or nut meats

Cooking Instructions :

Cream shortening and sugar; add eggs, orange juice, peel, vanilla,
and sour milk; mix well.
Add sifted dry ingredients. Add dates or nut meats.
Drop from teaspoon onto greased cookie sheet.
Bake in moderate oven (350°) 15 minutes.

Makes 5 dozen cookies.

Notes :

From the mess hall from one of our Veteran friends.

DIFFICULTY:

RATING:

PREP TIME:

COOK TIME:

Ingredients:

1 ½ sticks of melted butter
2 ½ c. chopped pretzels
3 Tbsp. sugar

Blend by hand next three:
8 oz. cream cheese
8 oz. cool whip
1 c. sugar
1 lg. box raspberry Jell-o
1 ½ c. boiling water
2 – 10 oz. pkg of frozen raspberries

Cooking Instructions :

Mix first three ingredients to form crust.
Blend cream cheese, cool whip and sugar.
Spread on cooled crust.
Mix Jell-O powder and boiling water until dissolved.
Add frozen raspberries until thawed.
Pour over second layer and refrigerate.

Notes :

From the mess hall of Shirley Merrill.

Recipe : Peach Cobbler III

DIFFICULTY:

RATING:

PREP TIME:

COOK TIME:

Ingredients:

¼ c. butter
½ c. white sugar
1 c. all purpose flour
¼ tsp. salt
2 tsp. baking powder
2 c. fresh peaches, pitted and sliced
¼ c. white sugar

¼ tsp. ground cinnamon
1 ½ c. water
½ c. milk

Cooking Instructions :

In large bowl, cream the butter and ½ c. sugar
In separate bowl, mix flour, salt, baking powder. Add the
Creamed mixture alternately with the milk.
Spread mixture evenly into baking dish. If using canned peaches,
drain thoroughly, reserving the juice. Spoon fruit over batter.
Sprinkle with cinnamon and ¼ c. sugar. Pour fruit juice or water
over the top.
Bake at 375 for 45 to 55 minutes. During baking the fruit and juice
go to the bottom and the batter rises.

Preheat oven to 375. Lightly butter 9x9 glass baking pan.

Notes :

From the mess hall of Shirley Merrill.

Recipe : Poor Man's Chocolate Cake

DIFFICULTY:

RATING:

PREP TIME:

COOK TIME: 30-35 minutes

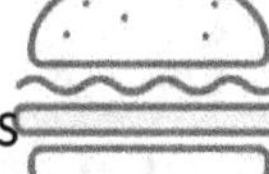

Ingredients:

1 ½ c. sifted flour
1 c. sugar
½ tsp. salt
3 T cocoa
1 tsp. baking soda

6 T oil
2 T white vinegar
1 T vanilla
1 c. water

Cooking Instructions :

Sift dry ingredients together directly into a 8x8x2 ungreased
cake pan.
Add the oil, vinegar and vanilla.
Pour in the water and mix thoroughly with fork.
Bake in a 350 degree oven for 30-35 minutes.

Notes :

From the mess hall of Pat Salmon.

Recipe : Pumpkin Bread

DIFFICULTY:

RATING:

PREP TIME:

COOK TIME:

Ingredients:

2 c. sugar
1 c. salad oil
3 eggs – add one at a time
2 c. pumpkin
3 c. flour
½ tsp. soda

½ tsp. salt
1 tsp. cloves
1 tsp. cinnamon
1 tsp. nutmeg

Cooking Instructions :

Mix first three items with a mixer until incorporated.
Add in all the other ingredients mixing between each addition.

Put in two loaf pans. Bake at 350 for 1 hour.

Notes :

From the mess hall of Jane Hallowell. Submitted by Michelle Libby

Recipe : Pumpkin Whoopie Pies

DIFFICULTY:

RATING:

PREP TIME:

COOK TIME:

Ingredients:

2 c. brown sugar
1 c. vegetable oil
1 ½ c. cooked, mashed pumpkin
2 eggs
3 c. flour
1 tsp. salt
1 tsp. baking powder

1 tsp. baking soda
1 tsp. vanilla
1 ½ tbsp. cinnamon
½ tbsp. ginger
½ tbsp. ground cloves

Cooking Instructions :

Cream sugar and oil.
Add pumpkin and eggs. Add flour, salt, baking powder,
soda, vanilla and spices.
Mix well.
Drop by heaping teaspoons onto greased cookie sheet.
Bake at 350 for 10 – 12 minutes.
Make sandwiches from 2 cookies filled with the whoopie pie
filling recipe.

Notes :

Filling:
1 egg white, beaten
2 tbsp. milk
1 tsp. vanilla
1 c. powdered sugar

Mix, then add 1 more cup
Powdered sugar and
¾ c. shortening.

Delivered by Pam Whynot.

Recipe : Rhubarb Pie

DIFFICULTY:

RATING:

PREP TIME:

COOK TIME:

Ingredients:

3 tbsp. flour
1 c. sugar
1 egg beaten
2 c. rhubarb cut into small pieces
½ tsp. salt

Optional: add strawberries
Add: 1/3 c. flour
Dash salt

Cooking Instructions :

Sift flour, sugar and salt together. Add egg and beat thoroughly, add rhubarb. Line pie pan with pastry and pour in filing. Cover with top with crust. Bake in hot oven 425 for 10 minutes.
Reduce heat to 350 and bake 35 minutes longer.

If you add strawberries: Add them to rhubarb ingredients and bake at 400 for 50 to 55 minutes.

Notes :

From the mess hall of Donna Cote. Submitted by Shirley Merrill.

<table>
<tr><td>Recipe :</td><td>Southern Cream Cookies</td></tr>
</table>

DIFFICULTY:

RATING:

PREP TIME:

COOK TIME: 15 minutes

Ingredients:

1 c. shortening
2 c. sugar
3 well-beaten eggs
1 tsp. vanilla extract
1 c. sour cream
5 c. flour
1 tsp. salt

3 tsp. baking powder
½ tsp. soda
1 ½ c. broken walnut meats
3 T sugar
1 tsp. cinnamon

Cooking Instructions :

Cream shortening and 2 cups sugar; add eggs; vanilla, and sour cream; mix well. Add flour sifted with salt, baking powder and soda. Add nut meats. Drop from teaspoon onto greased cookie sheet. Grease bottom of small glass; dip into mixed sugar and cinnamon; press cookie flat. Bake at 350° for 15 minutes. Makes 6 dozen cookies.

Notes :

From one of our veteran friends.

Recipe : Sugar Cake

DIFFICULTY:

RATING:

PREP TIME:

COOK TIME: 30 minutes

Ingredients:

1 c. all purpose flour
2 tsp. baking powder
1 tsp table salt
1 tsp vanilla extract
½ c. oil

1 large egg in a glass measuring cup & add milk to fill the measuring cup to a full 1 cup.

Cooking Instructions :

Bake in a 8x8 inch square pan or a 9x9 inch square pan (greased and flour pan before putting in cake batter).

Bake at 350° for 30 minutes. Cool before taking out of pan. Frost with a butter icing or sprinkle confectionery sugar on top.

Notes :

From the mess hall of Anne Cummings. Wife of Clarence Cummings, retired U.S. Army.

Recipe : Sugar-Free Apple Pie

DIFFICULTY:

RATING:

PREP TIME:

COOK TIME: 50 minutes

Ingredients:

5 large apples, peeled and cored
½ tsp. cinnamon
¼ tsp. nutmeg
2 T vegetable oil

¾ c. unsweetened apple juice concentrate
2 (9inch) crusts
2 ½ T tapioca

Cooking Instructions :

Preheat oven to 350°. In a large bowl, stir together sliced apples, cinnamon, nutmeg, tapioca, oil, and apple concentrate. Allow mixture to sit for 10 minutes. Pour mixture into pie crust and add top crust. Seal edge of pie crusts and slit top crust. Bake 1 hour or until top is brown. Cool before serving. Serve warm or cold. Refrigerate leftover pie.

Notes :

From the mess hall of Mildred Black.

Recipe : Stay up all night cookies

DIFFICULTY:

RATING:

PREP TIME:

COOK TIME:

Ingredients:

2 egg whites
2/3 c. sugar
½ tsp. vanilla
6 oz. chocolate bits

Cooking Instructions :

1. Beat 2 egg whites (at room temperature) until very stiff.
2. Add 2/3 c. sugar and ½ tsp. vanilla
3. Beat until stiff.
4. Fold in 6 oz. chocolate bits/chips
5. Preheat oven to 375 degrees. Put cookies in oven and turn
Off oven. Leave overnight. Don't open the oven!

Notes :

From the mess hall of Pam Whynot.

Recipe : Raw Apple Cake

DIFFICULTY:

RATING:

PREP TIME:

COOK TIME: 1 hour

Ingredients:

1 Stick butter
2 c. Sugar
2 Eggs

Sift together:
2 c. Flour

1 tsp. Baking soda
½ tsp. salt
1 tsp. cinnamon
1 tsp. vanilla
4 c. Raw apples (skinned and diced))
1 c. Chopped nuts

Cooking Instructions :

Mix the sifted ingredients to the cream. Add vanilla, apples and nuts.
Pour into a greased 9x13 inch pan.
Bake at 350 degrees for about 1 hour.

Notes :

From the mess hall of Shirley Merrill.

<table>
<tr><td>Recipe : Southern Pecan Pie</td><td>DIFFICULTY:
RATING:
PREP TIME:
COOK TIME:</td><td></td></tr>
</table>

Ingredients:

¼ c. butter soften
¾ c. sugar
1 tsp. vanilla
3 eggs beaten well
1 c. dark corn syrup
1 ½ c. pecan halves
9" unbaked pie shell

Cooking Instructions :

Cream butter and sugar. Gradually add next three ingredients.
Sprinkle peakon halves in pie shell. Pour fillings over all.
Bake in preheated 450 oven for 10 minutes.

Reduce heat to 350, make 30 to 35 minutes until the pie sets.

Notes :

From the mess hall of Shirley Merrill.

Recipe : Strawberry fluff

DIFFICULTY:

RATING:

PREP TIME:

COOK TIME:

Ingredients:

12 oz. frozen strawberries sliced
10 oz. mini marshmallows

Cooking Instructions :

Mix above and set overnight.
In the morning fold in real whipped cream, not Cool Whip.

Notes :

From the mess hall of Nina Braley.

Recipe : Tea Scones

DIFFICULTY:

RATING:

PREP TIME:

COOK TIME:

Ingredients:

3 cups flour
½ cup sugar (Splenda)
2 ½ tsp baking powder
½ tsp baking soda
1 tsp salt
¾ c. shortening (butter or Crisco)

¾ c. raisins (we also like to use Craisins)
1 c. buttermilk (or 1 c. milk & 1 T white vinegar)

Cooking Instructions :

Blend all the dry ingredients; cut in ¾ cups shortening; add ¾ cup raisins (or craisins); knead a little on a floured board; flatten to about ¾" thick; cut out with cookie cutter (or cut into triangles); brush top with milk
Bake at 375° for 15 minutes.

Notes :

From one of our Veteran friends.

Recipe : Vegan Orange Cake

DIFFICULTY:

RATING:

PREP TIME:

COOK TIME: 35 minutes

Ingredients:

1 ½ c. flour
1 c. sugar (< 1T)
1 tsp. baking soda
1/8 tsp. salt
1 c. orange juice
1/3 c. vegetable oil (little less)

1 Tbsp. grated orange zest
1 Tbsp. cider vinegar
1 tsp. Vanilla

Cooking Instructions :

In a large bowl, whisk first four ingredients.
In another bowl, mix all wet ingredients.
Combine together just until blended.
Bake at 350° in a greased and floured 8x8 pan for 30-35 minutes.

Notes :

From the mess hall of Jeanne Fiske.

Recipe : Whirligig Cookies

Ingredients:

½ c. Crisco
½ c. white sugar
½ c. brown sugar packed
½ c. peanut butter
1 egg
1 ¼ c. flour
½ tbsp. soda

½ tsp. baking powder
½ tsp. vanilla
½ tsp. almond extract
2 c. chocolate chips

Cooking Instructions :

Cream together first four ingredients.
Add egg, beat well. Add four and baking soda, baking powder
and vanilla. Mix all together.
Chill in refrigerator for approx. ½ hour. Roll dough into oblong
¼ inch thick on floured board.
Melt 2 c. chocolate chips and spread over rolled dough.
Roll up like jelly roll. Chill and slice ¼ inch thick.

Notes :

Bake at 375 on ungreased pan for 10 to 12 minutes.

From the mess hall of Gail Labbe.

Recipe : Whoopie Pies

Ingredients:

3 c. sugar
1 c. butter
4 eggs
½ c. vegetable oil
1 tbsp. vanilla
6 c. flour
2 c. unsweetened cocoa

1 tsp. baking powder
1 ½ tbsp baking soda
1 tsp. salt
3 c. milk

Filling: 1 ½ c. Crisco, 3 c. confectioners sugar, 1 1/3 c. marshmallow topping, dash salt, 1 tsp. vanilla extract, 1/3 to ½ c. milk

Cooking Instructions :

In a large bowl with an electric mixer, beat sugar, butter and eggs until combined. Add oil and vanilla.
Add dry ingredients a little at a time, mixing it regularly and adding 1 ½ c. milk and beat again.
Add remaining dry mixture and beat until it's all mixed. Add last 1 ½ c. milk and mix again. With a large scoop or spoon, drop the batter onto a baking sheet making it the size you choose.
Bake at 350 for 10 to 12 minutes. Let cool.
Filling: Add all ingredients and mix with a mixer. Add milk a little at a time until creamy.

Notes :

I double the filling recipe and usually add more confectioner's sugar to the filling to make it sweeter. These freeze well. This recipe makes a lot of whoopie pies.

From the mess hall of Michelle Libby.

Recipe : Whoopie Pies

DIFFICULTY:

RATING:

PREP TIME:

COOK TIME:

Ingredients:

1 egg	¼ tsp. salt
1 c. sugar	1 tsp. vanilla
5 Tbsp butter	FROSTING:
1 c. milk	½ to ¾ c. Crisco
5 Tbsp. cocoa	¾ c. confectioner's sugar
2 c. flour	3 tbsp. marshmallow
1 ¼ tsp. baking soda	1 tsp. vanilla

Cooking Instructions :

Mix all together. Spoon on to pan, like cookies
Bake for 10 minutes on greased pan at 360.

Whip frosting ingredients together.
Make sandwiches when cookie parts are cooled.

Notes :

From the mess hall of Colleen. Donated by Shirley Merrill.

Recipe : Woopie pies

DIFFICULTY:

RATING:

PREP TIME:

COOK TIME:

Ingredients:

6 tsp. shortening
1 egg
1 tsp. vanilla
2 c. flour
1 tsp. salt
1 c. sugar

1 c. milk
5 tbsp. cocoa
1 ¼ tsp. baking soda

Filling: combine 1+tbsp water,
½ c. sugar, 2/3 c. Crisco,
1/3 c. can evaporated milk.

Cooking Instructions :

Cream together shortening and sugar, add egg, milk, vanilla.
Blend in cocoa, flour, soda and salt. Drop by tbsp. on ungreased pan.
Smooth.
Bake in pre-heated 425 oven for 10 minutes.

Filling: Beat all ingredients with mixer at high speed until thick,
about 10 minutes.

Notes :

From the mess hall of Violet Marr. Submitted by Shirley Merrill.

Recipe : Wowie Cake

DIFFICULTY:

RATING:

PREP TIME:

COOK TIME: 30 minutes

Ingredients:

1 ½ c. all purpose flour
1 c. cold water
1 tsp. baking soda
½ tsp. table salt
1 tsp. white vinegar
1 tsp. vanilla extract

¼ c. cocoa
1/3 c. salad oil

Cooking Instructions :

Beat all ingredients together with and electric beater for 2 to 3 minutes before pouring into pan.

Bake at 350° for 30 minutes in a greased and floured 9x9 inch cake pan. May serve warm without frosting. Cool before slicing.

Notes :

From the mess hall of Anne Cummings. Wife of Clarence Cummings, retired U.S. Army.

Recipe : Zucchini cake with Sour Cream Frosting

DIFFICULTY:

RATING:

PREP TIME:

COOK TIME:

Ingredients:

2 medium zucchini
2 ¼ c. all purpose flour
1 ¼ c. sugar
1/3 c. shortening
½ c. milk
2 tsp. baking soda
½ tsp. salt

½ tsp. ground cinnamon
¼ tsp. nutmeg
¼ tsp. cloves
2 eggs
1 ¼ c. walnuts, chopped.

Cooking Instructions :

In covered blender or food processor with knife blade, blend zucchini until smooth. (1 ½ c. pureed.)
Preheat oven to 350. Grease 13x9 pan.
In large bowl, measure pureed zucchini, flour and remaining ingredients except walnuts. With mixer at low speed, beat ingredients until mixture is smooth. Stir in walnuts.
Pour batter into prepared pan. Bake 30 to 35 minutes. Cook cake completely in pan on wire rack.

Notes :

Half a cup of nuts is plenty, if you're not psyched about them.

From the mess hall of Shirley Merrill.

Other delights

Recipe : Canned Gingered Pears

Ingredients:

5 pounds firm, ripe pears, cored, peeled and quartered
½ c. lemon juice
1 tbsp grated lemon rind
½ c. minced fresh ginger root

Cooking Instructions :

Combine all ingredients in a large kettle and simmer until pears are translucent. Ladle into jars, adjust lids and process for 35 minutes. (If pears require sweetening when served, sprinkle with sugar substitute.

Makes 4 pints

Notes :

Donated by Alola G. Morrison, Army Reserve and Public Health

Recipe : Cinnamon Honey Syrup

DIFFICULTY:

RATING:

PREP TIME:

COOK TIME:

Ingredients:

1 c. sugar
2/3 c. water
¼ c. honey
1 sm. Cinnamon stick
1 tsp. fresh lemon juice

Cooking Instructions :

Mix all ingredients together and simmer for 30 minutes.
Cook until lightly brown.
Serve warm or cold.

Notes :

From the mess hall of Alola G. Morrison, Army Reserve and Public Health

Recipe : Canning Peach Chutney

DIFFICULTY:

RATING:

PREP TIME:

COOK TIME:

Ingredients:

1 c. vinegar
1 c. currants
2 tsp. salt
1 tsp. ginger
¼ tsp. cayenne pepper
4 pounds peaches, peeled, pitted
and chopped to 8 cups.

2 green peppers, seeded and
chopped
1 c. golden raisins

Cooking Instructions :

Treat peaches with ascorbic acid to prevent browning.
In a 5-quart Dutch oven, combine vinegar, currants, salt, ginger and
cayenne pepper. Heat to boiling, mixing well.
Stir in peaches, peppers and raisins. Boil mixture gently until it thickens
(45 min.) Spoon into clean jars, adjust lids and process for 15 minutes
after water comes to a boil.

Makes 4 pints

Notes :

Donated by Alola G. Morrison, Army Reserve and Public Health

Recipe : Chocolate Oatmeal Cookies

DIFFICULTY:

RATING:

PREP TIME:

COOK TIME: 10-12 min.

Ingredients:

1 c. sugar
1 c. brown sugar
1 ½ sticks butter
2 lg. eggs
2 c. all-purpose flour
¼ c. cocoa
1 tsp. baking soda

½ tsp. salt
¼ c. water
2 c. rolled oats

Cooking Instructions :

Cream sugars and butter together at medium speed until light and fluffy. Add eggs and vanilla and beat at medium speed until creamy. Scrap the bowl.

In another bow., stir flour, cocoa, baking soda, baking powder and salt together. Add to creamy mixture. Mix a medium speed until four is moistened. Add water and oats. Mix at medium speed until oats are absorbed into the dough.

Drop dough by tablespoon onto cookie sheets lined with foil.

Notes :

Bake at 375 degrees for 10-12 minutes or until centers of cookies are almost firm. Leave cookies on the sheets for 3 to 4 minutes, then place on wire rack to cool at room temperature.

Makes 48 cookies.

Recipe : Cole Farm Salad Dressing

DIFFICULTY:

RATING:

PREP TIME:

COOK TIME:

Ingredients:

1 can tomato soup
1 c. sugar
½ salad oil
½ c. salad oil
½ c. vinegar
1/8 c. (2 tbsp.) water

½ tsp. garlic powder
Pinch salt

Cooking Instructions :

Blend all ingredients together.
Makes 1 quart.
Place in a quart canning jar with a lid. Keep chilled in refrigerator.
Serve over tossed salad, sliced cukes, tomatoes, lettuce, etc.

Notes :

From the mess hall of Alola G. Morrison, Army Reserve and Public Health.

Recipe : Cranberry Stuff

Ingredients:

3 c. diced fresh cranberries
1 med. Yellow onion – diced
1 c. + 2 Tbsp. reg. sour cream
½ c. + 2 Tbsp. sugar
3 tbsp. horseradish

Cooking Instructions :

Mix altogether and freeze.
Take out of freezer 1 hour before serving the turkey.

Notes :

Serves 8 to 10 people
From the mess hall of Joe Morrison. Submitted by his wife, Alola Morrison.

Recipe : Double Peanut Cookies

DIFFICULTY:

RATING:

PREP TIME:

COOK TIME: 12 min.

Ingredients:

½ stick margarine
1 c. sugar
½ c. peanut butter
1 tsp. vanilla
¼ c. water
1 ¼ c. flour
½ tsp. baking soda

½ tsp. salt
1 c. chopped roasted peanuts

Cooking Instructions :

Cream margarine, sugar and peanut butter together until light and fluffy. Add vanilla and water, and mix at medium speed for 1 minute.
In a separate bowl, stir flour, baking soda, salt, and peanuts together and add to creamy mixture. Mix to blend.
Drop dough by 1 ½ tablespoonfuls onto cookie sheets.
Bake at 350 F for 12 minutes or until lightly browned. Leave cookies on sheets for about 3 minutes. Remove and place on wire rack to cool.

Notes :

Makes 24 cookies.

From the mess hall of one of our Veteran friends.

Recipe : Honey Butter

Ingredients:

½ c. soft butter or margarine at room temperature
½ c. honey
1 tsp. cinnamon

Cooking Instructions :

Blend ingredients together.
Spread over toast, biscuits, English muffins, etc.

Notes :

From the mess hall of Alola G. Morrison, Army Reserve and Public
Health

Recipe : Herbal Garlic Butter

DIFFICULTY:

RATING:

PREP TIME:

COOK TIME:

Ingredients:

1 tsp. basil
¼ tsp. Thyme
½ tsp. tarragon
2 tsp. parsley
½ tsp. grated lemon peel
1 clove garlic, crushed

1 onion, chopped fine
Dash cayenne pepper
Dash salt
½ c. soft butter or margarine

Cooking Instructions :

Combine all ingredients except butter with a wooden spoon and mix together.
Add butter.
Serve over hot vegetables or spread over French bread slices.

Notes :

From the mess hall of Alola Morrison's mother-in-law, Arnetta Morrison.

Recipe :

Lemon Licorice Cookies

DIFFICULTY:

RATING:

PREP TIME:

COOK TIME: 12 to 15 min

Ingredients:

1 ½ sticks margarine
¾ c. cry, sweetened lemonade mix
¼ c. sugar
1 tbsp. anise seed or anise flavoring
¼ c. water
¼ c. egg whites
3 c. flour

¼ c. instant dry milk
1 tsp. baking soda
½ tsp. salt

Cooking Instructions :

Cream margarine, lemonade mix, sugar and anise seed together at medium speed until light and fluffy. Add water and egg whites. Mix at medium speed for 30 seconds scraping the bowl at times.
In another bowl, stir flour, dry milk, soda and salt. Add to creamed mixture and mix to blend.
Drop dough by 1 ½ tablespoonfuls on cookie sheets. Press each cookie down with the back of a tablespoon dipped in cold water.

Notes :

Bake at 350 for 12 to 15 minutes or until lightly browned.
Place on wire rack to cool.
Makes 36 cookies.

From one of our Veteran friends.

Recipe : Mock sour cream

DIFFICULTY:

RATING:

PREP TIME:

COOK TIME:

Ingredients:

1 c. skim ricotta cheese
½ c. skim ricotta cheese
½ c. buttermilk
2 tbsp. fresh lemon juice
2 tsp. Worchester sauce

Cooking Instructions :

Using food processor, mix the ingredients until blended smooth.
Store in a lidded jar in the refrigerator for up to 1 week.
Serve over salad.

Notes :

From the mess hall of Alola G. Morrison, Army Reserve and Public
Health

Recipe : Nut and Cereal Cookies

DIFFICULTY:

RATING:

PREP TIME:

COOK TIME: 12 to 14 min.

Ingredients:

1 c. oat bran cereal	2 sticks margarine	½ c. water
1 c. Fiber One cereal	2 tsp. vanilla	
1 c. bran flakes	2 large eggs	
1 c. rolled oats	2 c. flour	
1 c. seedless raisins	1 tsp. baking powder	
1 c. chopped walnuts	1 tsp. baking soda	
1 c. brown sugar	½ tsp. salt	

Cooking Instructions :

Combine oat bran cereal, Fiber One, bran flakes, rolled oats, raisins and walnuts in a bowl, mix lightly. Set aside.

Cream brown sugar and margarine at medium speed until light and fluffy. Add vanilla and eggs. Mix at medium speed for 1 minute scraping down the bowl.

In another bowl, stir flour, baking powder, baking soda and salt together and add to creamed mixture. Add water. Mix only to blend and add reserved cereal mixture. Mix until blended. Put on cookie sheet in 1 ½ tablespoonfuls.

Notes :

Bake at 375 for 12 to 14 minutes or until lightly browned. Cool on wire rack. Makes 48 cookies.

From the mess hall of one of our Veteran friends.

Recipe : Nut Salad Mix

DIFFICULTY:

RATING:

PREP TIME:

COOK TIME:

Ingredients:

1 Crunchy Topping for salads or
vegetables
2 pkg. ramen noodles crushed (take
out the seasoning packet.)
3 Tbsp. sesame seeds or sunflower
seeds
1 pkg. slivered almonds

½ c. margarine, melted
1 tsp. garlic powder

Cooking Instructions :

Melt margarine in a large frying pan. Stir in noodles and almond slivers,
garlic powder and sunflower seeds.

Stir constantly, flipping mixture over until light brown.

Cool and sprinkle over lettuce or tossed salad or cooked vegetables like
green beans.

Notes :

From the mess hall of Alola G. Morrison, Army Reserve and Public
Health

Recipe : Peanut Butter and Pumpkin Dog Treats

DIFFICULTY:

RATING:

PREP TIME:

COOK TIME:

Ingredients:

2 ½ c. whole wheat flour
2 eggs
½ c. canned pumpkin
2 tbsp. peanut butter
½ tsp. salt
½ tsp. ground cinnamon

Cooking Instructions :

Whisk together the flour, eggs, pumpkin, peanut butter, salt and cinnamon in a bowl. Add water as needed to help make the dough workable, but the dough should be dry and stiff. Roll the dough into a ½ inch thick slab.

Cut them in sticks or use creative cookie cutters and use the dough like you would sugar cookies.

Bake at 350 for 40 minutes.

Notes :

Submitted from the mess hall of Michelle Libby. Approved by Chloe the Dog.

Recipe : Pickled Tarragon Carrots

DIFFICULTY:

RATING:

PREP TIME:

COOK TIME:

Ingredients:

48 baby carrots
12 sm. white onions
½ c. pickling salt
8 hot green chili peppers
4 tsp. dried tarragon

20 peppercorns
2 bay leaves
1 pt. white wine tarragon vinegar

Cooking Instructions :

Place carrots and onions in a glass bowl with pickling salt and let stand for 24 hours.

Drain carrots and onions. Pack into clean jars with 2 hot peppers in each jar. Add to each jar 1 tsp. tarragon, 5 peppercorns and ½ by leaf. Fill jars with boiling tarragon vinegar. Seal and process for 30 minutes.

Makes 4 pints

Notes :

Donated by Alola G. Morrison, Army Reserve and Public Health.

Recipe : Roquefort Dressing

DIFFICULTY:

RATING:

PREP TIME:

COOK TIME:

Ingredients:

1 tsp. salt
½ tsp. dry mustard
½ tsp. black pepper
1 Roquefort cheese wedge broken
up
½ tsp. paprika

½ tsp. sugar
¾ c. oil
½ c. white vinegar

Cooking Instructions :

Mix together all ingredients and shake well.

Store in a jar and refrigerate until ready to use.

Notes :

From the mess hall of Alola G. Morrison, Army Reserve and Public
Health

Recipe : Salsa

Ingredients:

16 c. tomatoes, peeled and chopped
4 c. green peppers
4 ½ c. hot chili peppers
1 ½ c. jalapeno peppers, minced
4 c. chopped onion

3 Tbsp. salt
12 cloves garlic, minced
3 c. cider vinegar
¼ c. sugar

Cooking Instructions :

Place tomatoes, peppers and onion in a large kettle.

Add salt and garlic and cook until thick (2-3 hours).

Add vinegar and sugar and ladle into jars.

Seal and process for 35 minutes.
Makes 12 pints.

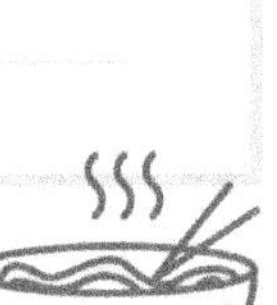

Notes :

Donated by Alola G. Morrison, Army Reserve and Public Health.

Master Mix

Recipe : Master Mix

DIFFICULTY:

RATING:

PREP TIME:

COOK TIME:

Ingredients:

9 c. sifted flour
4 Tbsp. baking powder
1 Tbsp. salt
1 1/3 c. non-fat powdered milk
3 sticks butter

Cooking Instructions :

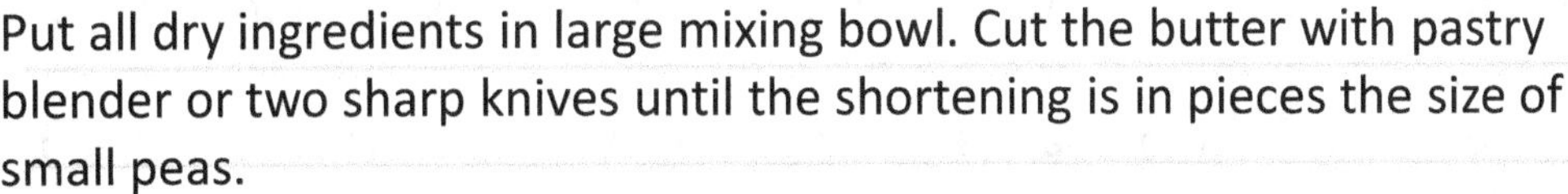

Put all dry ingredients in large mixing bowl. Cut the butter with pastry blender or two sharp knives until the shortening is in pieces the size of small peas.

Store in a tightly closed container. It keeps for several weeks in a cupboard. If lard is used as the shortening, it must be refrigerated.

Notes :

This is truly a homemade version of the pre-packaged mixes like Bisquick, Aunt Jemima and Krusteaz.
If you want to use a recipe from one of the boxes, add water instead of milk and do not add extra shortening except for shortcake and waffles, which need a little extra fat.

DIFFICULTY:

RATING:

PREP TIME:

COOK TIME:

Ingredients:

2 c. Master Mix
¾ c. water

Cooking Instructions :

Add liquid to mix carefully to form a stiff dough that can be removed from a bowl in a single lump.

Place dough on floured board and knead briefly using extra flour to keep dough from sticking.

Pat or roll dough into a ½ inch thickness and cut with a 2" biscuit cutter dipped in flour. Place biscuits on ungreased cookie sheet.

Bake at 425 degrees for 12 to 15 minutes, until lightly brown.

Variations

Buttermilk biscuits: 2 c. Master Mix, add ¼ tsp. baking soda, mix well and moisten with ¾ c. buttermilk

Cheese biscuits: 2 c. Master Mix, add 1 c. grated sharp cheddar cheese, mix well and proceed as above.

Cinnamon biscuits: 2 c. Master Mix, add 1 tsp. cinnamon and 3 Tbsp. sugar. Mix well and moisten with ½ c. water or milk into which 1 egg has been beaten. Proceed as above.

Recipe : Master Mix with Higher Protein

DIFFICULTY:

RATING:

PREP TIME:

COOK TIME:

Ingredients:

9 c. flour
2 c. non-fat dry milk powder
1 c. soy flour
1 c. wheat germ
5 ½ Tbsp. baking powder
1 ½ Tbsp. salt
3 sticks butter

Cooking Instructions :

Sift all dry ingredients except wheat germ.
Stir in wheat germ. Cut margarine with pastry blender until shortening
is in pieces the size of small peas.
Store in tightly sealed containers.

Notes :

Master Mix and recipes are from the mess hall of Home
Economists of Richmond, CA.

Recipe : Extra Special Hot Cakes

DIFFICULTY:

RATING:

PREP TIME:

COOK TIME:

Ingredients:

¼ c. Master Mix
1 Tbsp. non-fat dry milk powder
2 Tbsp. Yogurt, plain or flavored
2 Tbsp. cottage cheese
1 egg
¼ tsp. cinnamon
¼ tsp. ground cardamon

Butter for frying

Cooking Instructions :

Blend all ingredients in bowl until well mixed. Melt shortening on large skillet. Pour batter into hot pan to form three large pancakes. Fry on med. Heat until surface is covered in bubbles.
Turn with spatula. Brown well on other side.
Serve with Maine Maple Syrup.

Notes :

DIFFICULTY:

RATING:

PREP TIME:

COOK TIME:

Ingredients:

2 c. Master Mix
2 Tbsp. sugar
1 egg
¾ c. water

Cooking Instructions :

Mix all ingredients until well moistened.
Fill greased muffin cups 2/3 full.
Bake 15 minutes at 400 degrees

Notes :

Master Mix –
Pancakes

DIFFICULTY: 

RATING:

PREP TIME:

COOK TIME:

Ingredients:

2 c. Master Mix
1 egg
1 Tbsp. sugar (optional)
1 egg
¾ c. water

Cooking Instructions :

Blend mix, egg and water until mix is moist.
Melt shortening in large skillet or griddle. Pour batter onto hot skillet to form pancakes.
Fry until surface is covered with bubbles.
Turn with spatula. Brown well on other side.
Serve with Maine Maple Syrup.

Notes :

Recipe : Master Mix – Upside down cake

PREP TIME:

COOK TIME:

Ingredients:

2 c. Master Mix
1 egg
1 c. sugar
½ c. water

Topping:
2 Tbsp. melted butter
1 c. brown sugar
Slices for fruit such as pineapple, apple, cranberries, cherries or others.

Cooking Instructions :

Spread topping mixture and fruit into 8-inch baking pan. Over this spread the batter made from blending the master mi and other ingredients.
Bake at 400 degrees for 25 to 30 minutes
Allow cake to cool for about ten minutes. Invert onto serving platter.

Notes :

Recipe : Master Mix - Waffles

DIFFICULTY:

RATING:

PREP TIME:

COOK TIME:

Ingredients:

2 c. Master Mix
2 Tbsp. Melted butter or margarine or oil.
2 eggs, slightly beaten
1 ¾ c. water
1 Tbsp. sugar (optional)

Cooking Instructions :

Blend all ingredients thoroughly. Bake in hot waffle iron.
Makes about 5 waffles.

Notes :

Buttermilk waffles: Instead of water, use 2 c. buttermilk and ½ tsp. baking
soda.

Recipe : Master Mix - Orange-Cranberry Muffins

DIFFICULTY:

RATING:

PREP TIME:

COOK TIME:

Ingredients:

1 ¾ c. biscuit mix
2 Tbsp. sugar
3 Tbsp. grated orange rind
1 c. sliced fresh cranberries
½ c. chopped walnuts or pecans

1 egg slightly beaten
¼ c. water
½ c. orange juice
1/3 c. honey or Maine Maple Syrup

Cooking Instructions :

With a fork, thoroughly blend biscuit mix, sugar, orange rind, cranberries and nuts.

In a separate bowl, beat egg slightly and blend in water, orange juice and honey. Add egg mixture to dry ingredients and mix only enough to moisten.

Fill muffin cups 2/3 full and bake in 400 degree over for 20 to 25 minutes.

Notes :

My recipes

Recipe :

DIFFICULTY:

RATING:

PREP TIME:

COOK TIME:

Ingredients:

Cooking Instructions :

Notes :

Recipe :

DIFFICULTY:

RATING:

PREP TIME:

COOK TIME:

Ingredients:

Cooking Instructions :

Notes :

Recipe :

DIFFICULTY:

RATING:

PREP TIME:

COOK TIME:

Ingredients:

Cooking Instructions :

Notes :

Recipe :

DIFFICULTY:

RATING:

PREP TIME:

COOK TIME:

Ingredients:

Cooking Instructions :

Notes :

Recipe :

DIFFICULTY:

RATING:

PREP TIME:

COOK TIME:

Ingredients:

Cooking Instructions :

Notes :

Recipe :

DIFFICULTY:

RATING:

PREP TIME:

COOK TIME:

Ingredients:

Cooking Instructions :

Notes :

Recipe :

DIFFICULTY:

RATING:

PREP TIME:

COOK TIME:

Ingredients:

Cooking Instructions :

Notes :

Recipe :

DIFFICULTY:

RATING:

PREP TIME:

COOK TIME:

Ingredients:

Cooking Instructions :

Notes :

Recipe :

DIFFICULTY:

RATING:

PREP TIME:

COOK TIME:

Ingredients:

Cooking Instructions :

Notes :

Recipe :

DIFFICULTY:

RATING:

PREP TIME:

COOK TIME:

Ingredients:

Cooking Instructions :

Notes :

Cooking Hacks

Substitute for All-Purpose Flour, Enriched

Substitute for thickening. Instead of 1 c. all purpose flour use,
¾ c. cornmeal (coarse)
1 c. fine cornmeal
7/8 c. rice flour
5/8 c. potato starch flour
1 c. corn flour
1 c. barley flour
1 ¼ c. rye flour
1 1/3 c. oat flour

If a recipe calls for "melted" fat, you can use oil, corn or canola oil.

Instead of 1 cup self rising flour, use…
1 cup all-purpose flour and ½ to 1 tsp. baking powder

1 tbsp. hard chocolate, unsweetened brick = 3 tbsp. cocoa powder plus 1 tbsp. of fat

Using a ceramic stone for breads and pizza
1. Rub cornmeal over the top of stone before putting pan into cook
2. Never use detergent to clean
3. Do not soak in water before using it
4. Always place in a cold oven first
5. Do not use a scouring pad to clean. Use a plastic scraper and paper towel.

Index

Index

Index

Index

Index

Index